The Yunnan Cookbook

Annabel Jackson & Linda Chia

BLACKSMITH BOOKS

The Yunnan Cookbook
ISBN 978-988-16139-7-4

Published by Blacksmith Books
5th Floor, 24 Hollywood Road, Hong Kong
Tel: (+852) 2877 7899 • *www.blacksmithbooks.com*

Location photography by San Lin, *slin604@gmail.com*
Recipe photography by Trio Photo
Tableware supplied by Equip Asia, *www.equipasia.com*
Map by Katy Hung

Also by Annabel Jackson:

Wine-Life Lessons
Food Art
Modern Indian Cooking
World Food China
Taste of Macau: Portuguese Cuisine on the China Coast
Hong Kong, Macau and the Muddy Pearl
Street Cafe Vietnam
Vietnam on a Plate
Macau on a Plate

Contents

Introduction: South of the Clouds 11
Our Collaboration 13

PRESERVES 17
Preserved Mustard Greens. 18
Pickled Radish and Carrot with Cucumber 19
Chilli Chutney 20
Spicy Sour Roast Peppers 22

APPETISERS 23
Yunnan Dips 24
Spicy Peanut Sauce 26
Yunnan Ham Appetiser Platter 27
Yunnan on a Platter. 28
What's for Breakfast?. 30
Breakfast in a Tibetan Village 34

SALADS 37
Mint and Pomelo Salad. 38
Bai Cucumber Salad. 40
Dai Cucumber Salad. 41
Warm Tofu and Cabbage Salad 42
Apple and Walnut Salad 44
Pomelo & Pomegranate Salad with Chinese Cabbage. 45
Steamed Taro & Broccoli with Grated Carrot .46
Steamed Pumpkin with Walnut & Herb Salad. 48
Spicy Cabbage Salad 50
Chunky Tomato and Mint Salad 51

A Sichuan Boy in Search of Paradise 52

SOUPS 55
Spicy Dai Tomato Soup. 56
Bai Chicken Soup 58
Pork Rib & Radish Soup 59
Sour-Spicy Fish & Tomato Soup in Clay Pot. 60
Pork Broth with Yunnan Ham 62
Village Vegetable Soup. 62
Chicken & Foraged Mushroom Soup 63
The Flower Festival 64

EGGS 69
Egg and Tomato Bake. 70
Fried Tomato with Egg 72
Scrambled Egg with Spicy Pork 73
Steamed Egg with Preserved Vegetables. 73
Egg Rolls. 74
Steamed Egg with Shiitake Mushrooms 76
Bitter Melon & Celery Omelette. 77
Lunch in a Dai Village 78
Growing Grapes in Yunnan 82

MUSHROOMS 85
Bamboo Shoots with Shiitake and Wood Ear Mushrooms 86
Enoki Mushrooms with Spicy Soy Bean Paste 87
Yunnan Ham with Autumn Melon & Shiitake Mushrooms. 88
Porcini Mushrooms with Yunnan Ham & Green Chilli Peppers. 90
Stir-Fried Mushrooms with Asparagus Tips 91
Spicy Aromatic Mushrooms. 94
Spicy Tofu with Fresh Mushrooms 94

Mixed Mushrooms with Mustard Greens. 95
Foraging for Mushrooms 96

VEGETABLES 103
Fried Tofu in Egg Batter 104
Celery with Spicy Sliced Chicken 106
Fresh Soy Beans with Chilli & Star Anise 106
Fresh Soy Beans with Yunnan Ham 107
Steamed Pumpkin with Honey 107
Asparagus Stems & Broccoli Stalks with Spicy Pork Loin 108
Zucchini with Sliced Pork & Dried Shrimps. 110
Chinese Broccoli & Asparagus with Breast of Chicken. 112

VEGAN 113
Fried Crispy Lotus Root with Garlic. 114
Cabbage & Pumpkin with Tomato Salsa 116
Naxi Stir-Fried Potatoes with Pickled Vegetables 116
Chinese Cabbage with Dried Chillies 117
Fried Eggplant with Dried Chillies 118
Tofu with Chinese Cabbage 120
Potato & Yam with Crunchy Green Peppers 122
"Grandma's Potatoes" 123
The Bai Chef 124
Lunch at Fuxian Lake. 126

MEAT AND POULTRY 131
Aromatic Lemon Honey Chicken. 132
Braised Pork Belly with Bitter Melon 134
Pork & Water Chestnut Patties 135
Eight Treasures Chicken 136
Steamed Pork Balls on Banana Leaf 138

Pork Loin with Mustard Greens & Preserved Vegetables 139
Roast Pork Rib with Chilli Bean Paste 140
Pork Stewed with Autumn Melon 142
Stuffed Banana Leaf 143
Roasted Bell Peppers stuffed with Pork & Tofu. 144
Sliced Pork with Garlic Chives 146
Stir-Fried Pork with Jicama & Asparagus Stalks. 147
Twice-Cooked Pork Belly with Kumquats 148
"Toasted" Duck. 150
Shangri-La 152

YUNNAN HAM 157
Steamed Yunnan Ham with Taro and Tofu 158
Yunnan Ham with Eggplant and Capsicum. 160
Yunnan Ham stuffed Lotus Root 162
The Naxi Restaurant Owner. 164

FISH AND SEAFOOD. 169
Shrimps with Garlic Chives 170
Dai Grilled Fish with Lemongrass 172
Fish and Tofu Hot Pot 174
Fish with Lotus Root & Tofu in Clay Pot 175
Sauteed Fish with Dragon Fruit in Blacksalty Seeds 176
Spicy Salt Prawns 178
Steamed Fish with Spicy Soy Bean Paste 180
Pan-Fried Spicy Squid 181
The Farming Life 182

RICE AND NOODLES 187
Pineapple Rice 188
Dai Noodle Soup 190

Fried Rice Noodles with Chicken 191
Cold Rice Noodles with Chinese Celery & Cucumber Salad 192
Akha Red Glutinous Rice with Yunnan Ham. .194
Potato Rice 196
Egg Fried Rice 198
Noodles with Fried Pork 198
Noodles with Braised Beef 199
Cross the Bridge Noodles 200

SNACKS AND STREET FOOD 203
Potato Pancakes. 204
Pork-stuffed Potstickers 206
Pumpkin Pancakes 208
Steamed Pork Buns 210
Crispy Spring Onion Cakes. 212
Spring Onion Pancakes 213
Dinner at Gold Beach. 214

CHEESE 219
Fried Yunnan Goat Cheese with Tomato Salsa 220
Yunnan Ham with Broad Beans & Goat Cheese. 222
Goat Cheese with Peas and Snake Beans 224
The Wa Cheesemaker. 226

DESSERTS. 229
Red Bean and Sweet Potato Balls 230
Pumpkin & Black Glutinous Rice Soup 232
In the Nomau Xichang Market 234

Acknowledgements 240

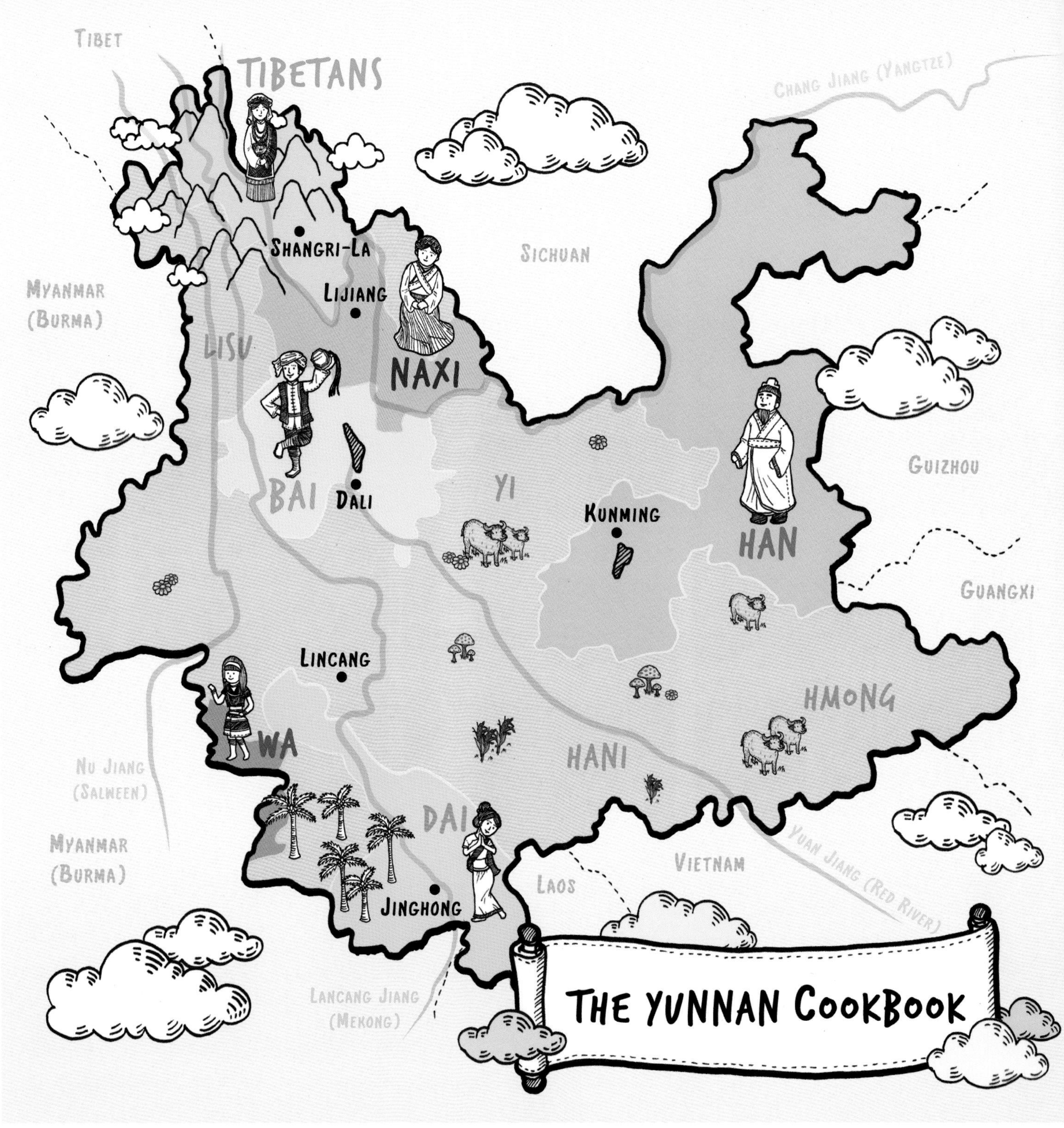
TIBET
TIBETANS
CHANG JIANG (YANGTZE)
SHANGRI-LA
SICHUAN
MYANMAR (BURMA)
LIJIANG
LISU
NAXI
GUIZHOU
BAI
DALI
YI
KUNMING
HAN
GUANGXI
LINCANG
HMONG
WA
HANI
NU JIANG (SALWEEN)
DAI
MYANMAR (BURMA)
VIETNAM
YUAN JIANG (RED RIVER)
LAOS
JINGHONG
LANCANG JIANG (MEKONG)
THE YUNNAN COOKBOOK

South of the Clouds

Within China, Yunnan inhabits a unique space. It borders the provinces of Guangxi, Guizhou, Sichuan and Tibet to the east and north, but its longest border, to the west and south, is shared not with another Chinese province but with Burma, and it also touches base with the northern parts of Vietnam and Laos.

The province is ethnically rich, agriculturally diverse and geographically highly contrasted. Each vista is as breathtaking as the next. The land moves from snow-covered mountains to some of the world's deepest gorges, active volcanoes and some almost bizarre formations such as the Stone Forest. There are deciduous and coniferous forests, and lush tropical jungles. That many mountains and trees (as well as animals and insects) are widely considered holy comes as no surprise.

Of a similar size to France (and with a similar range of regional cuisines), Yunnan is surely China's most glorious province. It is home to a wealth of flora and fauna, with many of the world's favourite flowers introduced from here. Of the 56 ethnic minorities formally recognised in China, 51 of them are represented in Yunnan (and 15 live exclusively here), and the otherwise dominant Han people (more than 90 per cent of the population of China) account for less than two-thirds of the population in this province whose name literally translates as "South of the Clouds."

It is a province of thrilling colour, too, and not only in the striking dress of some of the ethnic minorities who stick, still, to sartorial tradition – but also in its landscapes. Against a background of dark, brooding hills, brilliantly white cranes peck in brilliant green paddies under the sun's generous rays. Wild flowers abound roadside in shades of yellow, purple, blue and pink. Bright yellow rape fields extend to the horizon. Perfumed white peaches hang from low branches in orchards sloping gently towards lakes.

Not much grows at the high altitudes around Shangri-La, close to the north of the province on the borders of Tibet and Sichuan, where yak meat and yak products form the basis of the diet. But down south in Xishuangbanna, the produce is varied and decidedly south-east Asian; the markets of Jinghong city are a riot of colours and aromas. It is a similarly rich story in the province's capital city, Kunming, known as the City of Eternal Spring because of its temperate climate all year round, which results in a bounty of agricultural produce.

So it is hard to generalise about Yunnan cuisine. It almost doesn't exist, as each of the ethnic minorities have their own cooking traditions, and there's actually very little "Chinese" food on offer outside of Kunming – and even here it would incorporate local herbs, and chilli. The Cantonese might consider Yunnan food lacking in sophistication, and the average Sichuanese might judge it as lacking in flavour. In fact it probably sits somewhere between these two mighty gourmet traditions, with a Canton-esque emphasis on fresh produce but a Sichuan-esque predilection towards spice. Among the ethnic minorities, there are already widely differing attitudes to the amount of sour, salty and spice incorporated. However, the cooking of the Dai and the Naxi, the most easy to find because of copious restaurants in Jinghong and Lijiang respectively, are universally enjoyed.

If there is a culinary unifier within Yunnan, it is surely wild mushrooms, which emerge across the province in copious colours, shapes and sizes. These are eagerly and expertly (for many of them are toxic) foraged from wooded hillsides during the summer wet season. They are considered as nothing less than a gourmet treat; a pinnacle perhaps of the bounty which Yunnan generously provides for the dining table.

Our Collaboration

We're chatting about "blacksalty" seeds, which resemble fresh cracked pepper and have a smell about them which reminds me of sumac. To taste, they are a little sour, a little salty. What are they, I ask Linda. She explains that they're from an Akha village in Xishuangbanna, one of the most tropical and exotic parts of Yunnan Province. They are the dried seeds from a particular tree and, for Linda, represent a true Xishuangbanna flavour.

Help, I'm thinking, how many readers of our cookbook would have access to those? I suggest using sumac as a substitute. Linda says she would use black cardamom, another defining moment of Yunnan cooking (and unique to the province). How about we try a combination of the two? And so our conversation goes on.

Visiting Hong Kong, Linda was in a crowded noodle shop in the ultra-busy Causeway Bay district with a friend one lunchtime. An Italian couple sat down at the same table. "Could you help us order?" they said. The four got chatting, and Linda told Ugo and Chiara about some of the farming projects she was involved with in Yunnan Province. Ugo, an agronomist and part-time teacher with the Slow Food movement back home in Italy, was fascinated.

I had met Ugo just a week earlier through the international Slow Food network, and he and Chiara had already been over to my apartment on Kennedy Road, Chiara cooking the most fabulous gnocchi in a gorgonzola sauce, carbonara with pasta made from scratch, and surely the best tiramisu ever (and not only according to my son, Carlos).

"You must meet Annabel," said Ugo to Linda. "She's the convivium leader of Slow Food Hong Kong."

And so Linda and I met and immediately became friends.

Two months later I went to visit, flying with Linda from her then-home in Kunming to Jinghong, a charming city not far from the border with Myanmar. The weather was gorgeous, the people were attractive, and the wet market amazed me: full of the kind of produce I would buy when I had lived in Vietnam a decade earlier; far more southeast Asian than Chinese.

I was introduced to Dai food and immediately loved that: the raw dishes, the hot, the sour. In fact I was falling in love with the place, too. Linda and I talked about her projects, her achievements – and her dreams. A book featuring the cooking of the ethnic minorities needed to be written, but she didn't have time. Could I do it? Well Linda, with your help, yes!

I started travelling back and forth from Hong Kong to various parts of Yunnan, sometimes with Linda and sometimes alone, learning about the various cuisines and the unique culture of this colourful province. As we went forward, the cookbook started to become a real collaboration. My role would be mainly to write the book: the essays, the vignettes, and the actual recipes. I was already hanging out in kitchens, having cooking lessons, and testing recipes at home, but Linda's principal role would be to decide what dishes should be featured, and then cook them in our "test kitchen" in Hong Kong, where I weighed, watched, and wrote.

Linda is innovative, spontaneous and intuitive in the kitchen, basing her cooking on what ingredients are in the kitchen and not on a shopping list, without measuring and without recording anything. This part of the partnership, whereby I would record, would be critical. During the process, though, I did begin to see Linda writing things down!

We've researched as much as possible what ingredients are and aren't likely to be available to readers around the world, suggesting substitutes where possible. Not all the recipes are "authentic" – though, in the culinary world, that term is anyway highly controversial. Some of the recipes are based on the best of Yunnan ingredients, even if they are not traditionally cooked together. We wanted this book to bring Yunnan and its bounty to life, as well as presenting some of the best dishes to be experienced there.

Simple and traditional village cooking requires the finest and freshest of produce, which again we may not all have access to. Village cooking can look rustic at best, while we wanted to give the presentation a bit of an uplift. Linda is expert at presenting food on a plate, and I set about complementing her creations with photographic settings which would enhance her sense of colour. We picked out the palette of the dress of the ethnic minorities – shocking blues and pinks and greens; but also sparkling silver and textured black. The food photography, we hope, perfectly complements the location photography in this book, creating the broadest of landscapes.

– Annabel Jackson

Glossary

Some of the ingredients used in this book can be found under a range of different names. Here are some alternative names you might come across.

bitter melon	balsam pear / bitter gourd
capsicum	bell pepper
Chinese cabbage	Napa cabbage
coriander	cilantro / Chinese parsley
cornflour	cornstarch
eggplant	aubergine
glutinous rice	sticky rice
jicama	yam bean
kumquat	cumquat
lemongrass	citronella grass
mustard greens	mustard cabbage
papaya	pawpaw
peanut	groundnut
(white) radish	daikon
shrimp	prawn
Sichuan peppercorn	Chinese prickly ash / hua jiao
spring onion	green onion / scallion
tofu	beancurd / doufu
zucchini	courgette

PRESERVES

One of the many traditional practices observed by the peoples of Yunnan is the preservation of seasonal vegetables so that they can be eaten all year round. They consider that a vegetable preserved in season is superior to a vegetable grown at the wrong end of the season. At the height of the season, everywhere from village to city, people buy up radish, chillies, mustard greens and Chinese cabbage, and dry them in bamboo baskets under the sun. These preserves bring an important sour taste to many dishes – from breakfast noodles to clay pot fish.

Ready-made preserves are available everywhere from corner store to supermarket, because they're an important part of the Yunnan diet. However, more and more young people are now preparing them for themselves. If you're making chilli chutney at home, do be sure to open all the windows!

Preserved Mustard Greens

Mustard greens (*gai tsoi*) is available throughout the world, and is highly nutritious. It is brilliant as a little side dish. The drying process is traditionally carried out for about a week on bamboo trays, in the dry breeze. Here, the salt is the preserving agent. In Yunnan, less ginger is used as compared with other provinces of China, but the chilli component is higher.

INGREDIENTS

1 bunch mustard greens (about 3 stalks)
6 slices ginger
6 chillies
110 g / 4 oz salt
110 ml / 4 fl oz hot water
Water, for boiling

METHOD

1. Wash the stems and leaves and discard tough outer leaves. Dry
2. Slice stems, shred leaves, and put into a large saucepan
3. Bring a pan of water to the boil and blanch vegetables for ½ minute. Drain
4. In a sterilised jar, place ginger, chillies, salt and hot water
5. Add greens to the jar, and press thoroughly into the brine
6. Store in a cool, dark place. It is best after a few days

Pickled Radish and Carrot with Cucumber

When there is an excess at harvest, farmers and gardeners keep the best vegetables to preserve, to eat later with congee, steamed fish and pork. Traditionally, radish would be pickled alone, so this recipe is an adaptation. Linda can remember her (Cantonese) mother adding carrot. She continues this new "tradition" by adding her own new ingredient, the cucumber, which is so popular in Yunnan. She likes to pair this pickle with soya chicken.

INGREDIENTS

1 radish (about 500 g / 1 lb 2 oz), cut into strips
1 carrot, cut into strips
1 tsp salt
4 red chillies, chopped (the smaller the pieces, the more the flavours fuse)
450 ml / 1 pint white vinegar
1 cucumber, cut into strips

METHOD

1. Blanch the radish in very hot water for 1 minute
2. Stir in the carrot. Drain
3. Add salt, chillies, and enough vinegar to cover
4. Put in an airtight container and use after 1 week
5. Add cucumber just before serving

Chilli Chutney

Northern Yunnan people would add some chopped mint; the southern people would add chopped coriander. The chutney, on the right of the photo, is pictured with shop-bought preserved vegetables.

INGREDIENTS

250 g / 9 oz chillies, roughly chopped
1 head of garlic, cloves peeled and roughly chopped
2 tsp salt
2 tsp oil
2 tsp Chinese vinegar

METHOD

1. Pound chillies and garlic with mortar and pestle with salt until fused
2. Stir in oil and vinegar

Spicy Sour Roast Peppers

Traditionally, the vegetables would be barbecued over a raw flame, but they can be roasted in the oven. This condiment can be served immediately.

INGREDIENTS

1 red pepper, seeds removed, cut into quarters

1 green pepper, seeds removed, cut into quarters

2 red chillies

1 sour tomato, finely chopped, or 2 tsp vinegar

1 tsp salt

1 tsp pepper

METHOD

1. Heat the oven to 220°C / 440°F and roast the peppers, with the chillies, until blackened and soft and squishy
2. Remove the blackened skins
3. Mash the chillies with the peppers. Add tomato or vinegar, and then salt and pepper

APPETISERS

There's no obvious concept of appetisers in Yunnan eating. Dishes are made in rapid sequence, delivered to the table and only when the last dish is prepared do the guests sit down to dine. This means, indeed, that most dishes end up being eaten cold, even when we might imagine they would taste better hot.

The platters here make sensible appetisers if you want to divide the meal into courses. The dips and condiments can be left on the table throughout the meal.

Yunnan Dips

These are hugely flexible, and can be paired with everything from wild ferns to tofu to pieces of red meat. Vary quantities to suit your personal taste. (Pictured: Tomato Salsa; Spicy Peanut Sauce; Mint & Soy; Fermented Tofu & Soy).

TOMATO SALSA

1 tbsp finely chopped tomato
1 tbsp fresh tomato juice
1 tsp finely chopped mint
1 tsp finely chopped spring onion, green part
1 tsp finely chopped dried chilli
1 tsp vegetable oil
½ tsp salt
Juice of half a lemon
½ tsp black pepper
2 tsp finely chopped red onion
1 tsp finely chopped shallot

Mix together all the ingredients for a slightly chunky texture, or pound together for a smoother texture

SPICY SALT

1 tbsp rock salt
1 tsp Chinese five-spice
1 tsp dried chilli flakes
1 tsp black pepper

Combine all ingredients

MINT & SOY

1 tbsp light soy sauce
1 tbsp aged Chinese vinegar
2 tsp finely chopped garlic
1 tbsp finely chopped mint leaves

Combine all ingredients

FERMENTED TOFU & SOY

2 cubes fermented tofu
1 tbsp tofu liquid
2 tsp dried chilli flakes
2 tsp light soy sauce

Combine all ingredients or, for more fancy presentation, combine the liquids, pour over the tofu, and sprinkle with chilli flakes

SESAME OIL & SHALLOTS

2 tsp sesame oil
2 tsp light soy sauce
1 tsp finely chopped spring onion, green part

Combine all ingredients

Spicy Peanut Sauce

INGREDIENTS

200 g / 7 oz unsalted raw peanuts, with skins on

2 chillies

1 clove garlic

1 tbsp finely chopped mint leaves

1 tbsp finely chopped coriander leaves

2 tsp salt

1 tsp freshly ground black pepper

Hot water, as required

METHOD

1. Pan-fry the peanuts with about 1 tsp salt (the salt prevents them from burning) until the skins are crinkly and aromas emerge. Cool, and process to breadcrumb size. Set aside
2. Grill or roast the chillies, and grind in a pestle and mortar with the garlic. Add the herbs, 1 tsp salt and the pepper, and continue grinding
3. Add the peanuts. Slowly add hot water until the desired consistency is achieved: something similar to a satay sauce (or more liquid, as preferred)

Alternative recipe:

This peanut dip can also be made with split peas. Take 200 g / 7 oz split peas, soak them for 1-2 hours. Boil for 20 minutes. Cool. Process until still a little chunky, and then continue as for the peanut recipe.

Yunnan Ham Appetiser Platter

Yunnan ham is almost always cooked and used to flavour rather than as the main event. Here, we slice it very thinly, and suggest several dishes it can complement, offering a wonderful taste-test experience.

Here we have all the flavours of Yunnan, but presented with more than a hint of Italy. Think of it as prosciutto, and indeed substitute with prosciutto if you don't have access to Yunnan ham. Place little dishes of any of the Yunnan dips (see page 24) at the centre for extra interest.

SPICY ROASTED PEPPERS

Roast green and red peppers are deliciously sweet in Yunnan, where they are grilled over an open fire. They can also be prepared in the oven in the Italian manner until they are tender and the skin blackened. Cool. Place in a plastic bag and shake until the skins have peeled off. Sprinkle the flesh with chilli flakes.

PEACH AND PEAR COMPOTE

Halve each fruit and cook with a little sugar and cinnamon stick in enough water to just cover the fruit. Slice when cool.

CHINESE DUCK LIVER SAUSAGE AND PAPAYA

Different provinces in China produce different kinds of salami-style sausages, with the Cantonese *laap cheong* being perhaps the most famous. In the wet markets of Kunming, vendors add products like duck liver to substantially increase flavour. Such sausages are sliced and pan-fried with chilli flakes, then presented like salami. To echo these flavours, pan-fry duck and serve with the Yunnan ham slices, complemented not with melon but with papaya, a wonderful fruit from the south of Yunnan.

Yunnan on a Platter

Arrange various Yunnan dips (see page 24) on a platter and serve with all or some of the items mentioned here according to what's in season, and your personal preferences.

ASPARAGUS SPEARS

Wash and serve raw.

CUCUMBER

Discard the bitter ends of the cucumber, peel, and cut into strips. Remove seeds as necessary.

CABBAGE

Select an ultra-fresh (preferably organic), crispy round white cabbage. Quarter it, and break off leaves from the stem to dip.

TOFU

Cut into 4 cm / 1½ in square cubes and pan-fry in a non-stick pan for 1 or 2 minutes until golden brown. Dust with sea salt (or a mix of salt and Chinese five-spice), and serve cold.

CHICKEN

Use breast meat. Cut thin slices across the grain (to keep the meat tender) and pan-fry for a couple of minutes.

PORK

Pork is usually sold in China as skin, fat and meat all in one; just occasionally can one find a loin or a fillet, or even a belly rib. In the West, pork belly, once shunned, now appears on the menus of top restaurants.

PORK BELLY, LOIN AND FILLET

For pork belly, since the fat makes the meat tender, and the skin bears the flavour, how this piece is cut matters in order to maximise flavour and tenderness. Roast, then cut through the three component parts to serve. For loin and fillet, the browning (caramelising) process both tenderises and brings flavour. The manner of cutting depends on the dish, but for this platter, cut the belly across the grain into two-bite-sized pieces and pan-fry. For loin and fillet, finely slice across the grain and either pan-fry or, to be traditional, barbecue on skewers.

FISH

Choose a fish such as grass carp or ling. Slice it, but not too thinly. Mix crushed Sichuan peppercorns and salt and pepper with some corn starch, and lightly coat the slices. Fry in peanut oil in a very hot pan for about 2 minutes on each side until browned.

What's for Breakfast?

Noodles! There are essentially three kinds of rice noodles seen in Yunnan – fine round, medium round and flat, and many shops make their own. The texture can vary too.

Andrew Chen, who comes from Yiliang, went to boarding school in Kunming, just one hour away. But he never ate a single bowl of noodles in the capital, waiting until a visit home! "Noodles in Kunming have a strange texture," he says.

There may be subtle (or less-than-subtle to the experienced palate) variations in the pork broth, made with the bone off-cuts, and simmered overnight with spices such as star anise, cinnamon stick and black peppercorns. The intense flavour comes from the marrow in the bone. Make the broth at home. Throw in some cabbage or spinach, then put in the previously cooked dried noodles until they are warmed through.

This is the basic bowl, but then it's time for toppings, maybe as many as 20 choices in noodle shops across the province! These include chilli every way: flaked, freshly chopped, paste and so on. Herbs include chopped mint, coriander and chives, plus shredded Chinese cabbage, bean sprouts and finely chopped lalang grass rhizome. Soy sauce, vinegar, salt, MSG... There might also be braised beef, or stewed pork, and deep-fried bread sticks.

There's also a simple, vegetarian Naxi favourite, which tops noodles with tomato and egg, and then whatever is chosen from condiments of chive, soy, chilli flakes, fermented tofu, preserved vegetables, black vinegar and a touch of garlic. Plain and delicious, this is "cleansing" vegetarian food at its best.

But bread is also to be seen for breakfast, eaten in particular among the Muslim Hui minority, and at every street corner there's someone steaming *baozi*, selling 10 small buns per bag (even without stuffing). The Naxi people of Lijiang love bread too – the soft dough *shou rong bao* and the *bing*, served sweet with the essence of rose and black sesame, or savoury with a stuffing of salty Yunnan ham. And *baba* – which is basically the term for anything made of flour.

Twenty minutes outside Dali there is a village called Xizhou, and it is famous for *baba*. But this is not Naxi country. Rumour has it that a Naxi girl from Lijiang must have married a Bai boy from Dali and moved up here, and brought the *baba* recipe with her. Stuffed with spring onion and ground pork, the bread is filling, salty, and delicious. But, they'll say: it's still better back home in Lijiang. □

BREAKFAST IN A TIBETAN VILLAGE

Herds of Friesians, Jerseys and Guernseys graze in the muted green roadside paddocks, together with yak hybrids; and black piglets frolic while their minder sleeps on the grass, covered by a colourful embroidered drape, with her young daughter held close. They are the only humans to appear in the landscape for a while. To the right, crystal-clear water tumbles over rocks in the fast-moving brook which will eventually merge into the Yangtze. It is some 30 minutes outside Shangri-La, the road little more than a bumpy mud track, ruts filled with rainwater. It leads us to a Tibetan village populated by just 20 families.

Entry to the home is through imposing wooden doors into a courtyard where laundry flaps in the breeze. An elaborate staircase leads to the living quarters. The house is supported by the most enormous wooden beams of a breadth which could not be hugged by a normal-sized human. The trees are brought down from the mountainside with the aid of yaks, and require 15 men to lift them. What is not wood-carved is painted in typically colourful Tibetan flower motifs. Stepping over the hearth, one enters an ante-room which leads to the main living space. It is positively palatial. Every wooden carving conceals a cupboard, and the volume of pots and pans is incredible. How many people live here? There is a large kitchen, its main work surface covered in flour, together with a rolling pin. There is no bathroom.

Partaking of a meal which Tibetans have eaten for centuries, though these days it is eaten only for breakfast, has an air of ceremony about it. Seating is on a square, slightly raised stool set to one side of the elaborate, ornate, wood-burning stove, made of cast iron – every home has one as a centrepiece – whose smoke escapes through a narrow chimney stretching to the high roof, and coils around in July's cool morning air. Cone-shaped yak cheeses are placed on a wire rack above the stove, where they are air-smoked.

Serving breakfast is the family's 19-year-old daughter, a tall and elegant young woman in CK trainers (fakes?) who has recently married and works at the nearby upmarket Banyan Tree resort. It's probably that job which has lent her such poise. Grandfather is up in the mountains with the yaks – he will return in October – while her father works in construction in Shangri-La city to earn cash for the family. Her mother and grandmother take care of the family's agricultural land where they grow potatoes and buckwheat. Mother has been cutting fresh grass with a scythe, which will be dried and stored for the yaks to eat during the winter months, together with some barley. She has also been foraging for wild mushrooms, and she's smiling broadly as she enters the room: she has more than a kilo of Matsutake, which she can sell in the market, to a "businessman", for 200 yuan, and perhaps a smoked cheese, too, which can go for about 20 yuan. Another major source of cash is a mature, 400kg male yak which can sell for up to 10,000 yuan.

The first dish, gracefully presented, is a bowl of dirty-grey milled and toasted buckwheat; but the bowl is made from firwood and has a lovely grain. Yak butter tea is poured into pretty, colourful porcelain bowls. It's thick and oily, reminiscent of ghee, and prepared with green tea leaves and salt.

There's a plate of fluffy *baba* (bread) stuffed with pungent spring onion. Then comes the yak curd cheese braised in butter. There's a marvellous sweetness to the butter, suggesting that the yaks eat very well up there in the mountains. They love the mountain air. At altitudes of below 3,000 metres they become listless and prone to sickness.

When the tea is half finished, extra yak butter is added from the bowl of cheese, together with a couple of tablespoons of buckwheat flour. It is all mixed together by hand until it is thick, and then eaten. This, it emerges, is the traditional Tibetan *tsampa* "bread". The soft *baba* bread is only a recent addition to the diet, as are the spring onions stuffed inside it.

Yak milk is not particularly popular, but the butter and cheese made from it are mainstays.

Heavy rain is setting in as breakfast is finished, and back on the main road three girls huddle under a single umbrella. Aromas of Matsutake and smoked yak cheese fill the car as we head back to Shangri-La. ☐

SALADS

It is the salads, the majority from the Dai ethnic minority of Xishuangbanna, which perhaps most differentiates Yunnan's cuisine from the rest of China, and links the cooking with that of Southeast Asia, in particular Vietnam, Myanmar and to a certain extent Thailand. There is ubiquitous use of abundant local herbs, a love of the raw, and an insistence on a perfect sour-spice tang (though the Vietnamese use less chilli, and the Thais incorporate sugar).

Salads are ultimately refreshing – even to the point, sometimes, of being topped with ice.

Mint and Pomelo Salad

This is a classic Xishuangbanna salad, from a region of Yunnan where pomelos are sweet and mint plentiful. Vary the proportions of aromatic mint and chilli to taste.

The Dai people eat pomelo with green mango and chilli so, based on this concept, use sour and/or sweet fruit to suit your taste and to suit the season. If pomelo is unavailable, use grapefruit. This salad pairs well with fish.

INGREDIENTS

1 pomelo (or 2 grapefruit)
½ papaya (or other seasonal fruit)
2 tbsp coarsely chopped (or torn) mint leaves
2 tsp chilli flakes
1 tbsp apple cider vinegar
½ tsp salt

METHOD

1. Break the pomelo into small chunks, reserving any juice
2. Cut the papaya into small cubes
3. Toss the fruit and any juices with the other ingredients and serve

Bai Cucumber Salad

This refreshing cold dish comes from the Bai minority *ayis* (aunties), Cun Canlian and Hong Ruimei, who work miracles in the tiny kitchen inside Bivou, a gorgeous boutique hotel in Shuhe (a village outside Lijiang) with its own kitchen garden. The secret to this simple dish, though it has many mingling flavours, is to cleaver the cucumber and retain all the juices. Clearly organic cucumber works best.

INGREDIENTS

2 small cucumbers (about 200 g / 7 oz)
1 tsp light soy sauce
1 tsp rice vinegar
2 drops sesame oil
Pinch chilli powder
½ tsp finely minced garlic
Large pinch sea salt
½ tsp peanut oil
1 tsp vegetable oil
1 tsp crushed peanuts
½ tsp sesame seeds

METHOD

1. Smash the cucumber with a cleaver, scoring then hitting until it is roughly chopped
2. Mix the cucumber pieces with soy sauce, vinegar, sesame oil, chilli powder, garlic, salt and peanut oil
3. Heat the vegetable oil in a small pan, and pour over the cucumber mixture
4. Sprinkle peanuts and sesame seeds on the top. Serve at room temperature

Dai Cucumber Salad

The favourite Dai method would see ice stirred in before serving, to help crisp up the cucumber and keep the dish ultra-refreshing on a typically warm Jinghong evening. It is important that the cucumber has a good flavour and, so long as the seeds are soft, there is no need to remove them. The proportion of tomato should be about one part to nine parts cucumber.

This salad is a sophisticated version of street food.

INGREDIENTS

2 cucumbers, skinned and sliced thinly into about 1 cm x 3 cm / ⅓ in x 1 in
¼ tsp very finely chopped ginger
½ tsp very finely chopped garlic
Splash white vinegar
½ tomato, halved, seeds removed, and very finely sliced
1 tsp very finely chopped chilli
Salt, to taste

METHOD

1. Mix together cucumber, ginger, garlic and vinegar
2. Add tomato, chilli and a pinch of salt
3. Ice, if desired

Warm Tofu and Cabbage Salad

Chinese cabbage, known as *wong bok* or *wong nga pak* in Asian stores, is packed with nutritional value. It is one of the must-have vegetables in the Yunnan kitchen because it is so versatile. Served chilled on a hot summer's day, it has a fresh flavour like no other vegetable – and we have served it in its raw form so guests can taste its natural sweetness.

This flavourful dish was created in Jinghong. It is pleasing to the palate and to the eye with its colourful and contrasting taste of pickled carrots and the additional punch and crunch of the fried chillies. (Yes, Yunnan people eat whole chillies).

INGREDIENTS
200 g / 7 oz tofu
4 green chillies
4 red chillies
1 tbsp cornflour
50 g / 1¾ oz Chinese cabbage, shredded
100 g / 3½ oz pickled radish and carrots (see page 19)
2 tbsp corn oil, for frying

METHOD
1. Coat chillies with some of the cornflour. Heat the oil in a pan and fry them for 2 minutes until golden brown. Remove from oil and drain on kitchen paper. Reserve oil
2. Cut half the tofu into slices and half into cubes. Coat with the remaining cornflour and fry in the reserved oil on two sides until golden brown. Arrange the cubes on one side of a plate with the chillies and the slices on the other
3. Mix the cabbage and pickles together and place on top of the tofu slices

Apple and Walnut Salad

This is not a typical Yunnan salad, but one which perfectly reflects the produce of the Dali area, rich in walnuts, apple orchards, mint beds – and also a yoghurt producer. The harvesting and preparation of walnuts remains a community and family affair, the dexterity of those involved making quick work of the walnuts before they are delivered to the market. The red apples from this area are crunchy and not particularly sweet, so green apple may make a sensible substitute. So long as they are not dried out, the walnuts can be presented in halves. The proportion should be about half walnut to half apple.

INGREDIENTS

250 g / 9 oz walnuts, shelled, skinned and halved
2 apples
3 tbsp roughly chopped mint leaves
225 ml / 8 fl oz natural yoghurt
Salt and pepper, to taste

METHOD

1. Without peeling, chop the apples into pieces about the same size as the walnut pieces
2. Mix walnuts, apple and mint together. Lightly turn in the yoghurt, season with salt and pepper, and serve immediately

Pomelo & Pomegranate Salad with Chinese Cabbage

Drawing on Dai traditions, this recipe is Yunnan fusion, introducing the lovely tang of pomegranate, while substituting peanuts with the rather more sophisticated pine nut. Pomelo can be readily substituted with grapefruit, both yellow and pink.

INGREDIENTS

1 pomelo (or 2 grapefruit)
1 pomegranate
100 g / 3½ oz pickled radish (see recipe on page 19), chopped to the size of a pine nut
1 Chinese cabbage (the long, white one)
2 spring onions, chopped into pieces the size of a pine nut
100 g pine nuts, dry roasted in a pan (unless they are very fresh and crunchy)

METHOD

1. Break the pomelo into small chunks, reserving any juice
2. To separate the pomegranate seeds from the skin, cut the fruit in half and "tap" the seeds out
3. Using the stalks part only, cut the cabbage into little squares about 2 cm x 2 cm / ¾ in x ¾ in
4. Mix together pomelo (and juice), pomegranate, radish and cabbage
5. Top with spring onion and pine nuts just before serving

Steamed Taro & Broccoli with Grated Carrot

This is a quick, easy and nutritious warm salad with a lightly spicy salad topping.

INGREDIENTS

1 medium taro, cut into bite-sized pieces

1 head of broccoli, cut into florets

1 medium carrot, grated

1 tbsp chilli chutney (see page 20)

METHOD

1. Steam the taro for 10 minutes, top with the broccoli florets, and steam for a further 10 minutes
2. Mix together the carrot and chutney, and place on top of the steamed vegetables

Steamed Pumpkin with Walnut & Herb Salad

This dish is inspired by the iconic Dai dish of steamed pumpkin with honey, which is served cold; and the beautiful walnut farms in the northern parts of Yunnan. This a warm salad, served in the cavity of the pumpkin.

INGREDIENTS

½ butternut pumpkin
50 g / 1¾ oz walnuts
1 tsp salt
10 g / ¼ oz mint leaves, finely chopped
10 g / ¼ oz coriander leaves, finely chopped
1 tsp chilli chutney (see recipe on page 20)

METHOD

1. Slice a little skin off the bottom of the pumpkin to form a flat base so that it can stand in a steaming dish. Remove the seeds, and steam the pumpkin for 20 minutes
2. In a small pan, dry roast the walnuts with salt for 2 minutes. Shake off the salt. Toss the nuts with the mint and coriander. Reserve six nuts (for decoration) and roughly chop the remainder
3. Mix together the remaining mint and coriander with the chopped nuts. Stir in the chutney
4. Assemble in the pumpkin and top with whole walnuts

Spicy Cabbage Salad

Burma is just across the border from Yunnan's Xishuangbanna, and it is not unusual to find Burmese dishes in restaurants in this region. The ingredients of this salad reflect the similarity in agriculture, and also a love shared by the Burmese and the Dai people for the spicy-sour combination. The addition of fermented tea leaves adds an interesting earthy edge. The proportion should be about two-thirds cabbage to one-third cucumber.

INGREDIENTS

1 small round white cabbage, shredded
2 tomatoes
100 g / 3½ oz fermented tea leaves
6 chillies, finely chopped
2 tsp lime juice
1 cucumber, julienned
100 g / 3½ oz peanuts, roughly chopped
4 spring onions, finely chopped

METHOD

1. The tea leaves should be prepared in advance. Soak 3 tsp Chinese tea leaves in 1 tbsp hot water, and set aside for a week
2. Cut the tomatoes, remove the seeds and any liquid, and chop the flesh into small pieces
3. Mix together the tomato, tea leaves, chilli and lime juice
4. Toss with the cabbage and cucumber
5. Allow to stand for one hour to merge the flavours
6. Top with peanuts and spring onion just before serving

Chunky Tomato and Mint Salad

The ingredients of this dish are broadly Yunnan, but the practice of smashing them is very Dai. This, though, is a rough-chopped dish. The Dai are very keen on the combination of red onion and mint, rendered sour and thus refreshing by the addition of sour tomato. If your tomatoes are not sour, add 1 tsp fresh lime juice per tomato.

INGREDIENTS

2 tomatoes
1 red onion
2 chillies, finely chopped
40 g / 1½ oz roughly chopped (or torn) mint leaves
Pinch salt and pepper

METHOD

1. Quarter each tomato, then cut each quarter into three pieces, and place in a bowl. Add lime juice, if using, with chilli, salt and pepper
2. Chop the onion into chunks about half the size of the tomato pieces
3. Mix together tomato, onion and mint and serve

A Sichuan Boy in Search of Paradise

There's a chill in the air but the promise of sunray warmth later, as Chef Tony sets up for a cooking class by the pavilion overlooking the lagoon which is the heart of the Angsana Fuxian Lake resort.

He has worked here since 2012. On his table, a local green vegetable seems to have no English name, but he's also working with the young tip of the pine tree leaf which is identifiable, and looks somewhat similar to dill. The secret with those "tree" or wild tomatoes, he's saying, is to roast them first, to concentrate the flavour, and remove the skins afterwards. He's ever-so-carefully dissecting a strawberry – for garnish – into the finest slices you've ever seen. He's unpacking some frozen foraged mushrooms. *Frozen* foraged mushrooms? Yes. Even though we know when the foraging season is, some guests expect to have them all year round. New flash-freezing techniques give a pretty good result. Oh, and guests want them prepared with ingredients like foie gras these days. Which he does, and with aplomb. The textural balance is brilliant.

It was not always thus, this now-animated chef on stage, seamlessly cooking and talking. Perhaps the humour was, and the smiling was; but not this level

of technique, this knowledge, this market savviness – and a never-ending curiosity.

Tony Xiong arrived in Yunnan from Chongqing when he was 18 years old; ever since childhood, he had dreams of living in Yunnan. For him it represented a paradise and exuded a sense of mystery; not only because of Shangri-La but also because of what he had heard about Dali. He dreamed of four seasons and in particular the notion of spring. Such a contrast to the weather he was brought up with: a very cold winter followed by very hot summer. A lot of suffering.

Tony had never cooked in Chongqing, nor thought about it, and fell into the industry quite by accident. He first job was in a government-run three-star hotel. He spent the first year killing fish. In the second year, he was placed in charge of purchasing produce from the local market. Year three? Cooking rice. Next, *mise en place* until, finally, he got to cook cold dishes for a year. This gave him the chance to become a wok chef. In his 13th year, at the same hotel, he became the director of food and beverage. Not bad, he says, smiling (and he smiles a lot), for a boy who started out killing fish.

Has Yunnan lived up to his dreams? There was a bit of a false start when, having fallen in love with a girl from Sichuan, she abandoned him for a Yunnan boy after just one month. But yes, he loves the place. Shangri-La remains the most mysterious of all the cities he has visited in the province, but he can't say it is the most beautiful! And he loves the rich food culture and produce, especially the seasonal produce. Mushrooms May to September; flowers in spring; wild vegetables from the mountain. The climate has lived up to his expectations but, more than anything, he knows that Yunnan people really do have beautiful hearts. □

SOUPS

Simple cooking requires the very best ingredients – and nowhere is this better illustrated than through the experience of Yunnan village soups. They are as simple as it gets.

Fill a wok about three-quarters full of water. Heat. Add vegetables and cook until tender. Those vegetables are organic by definition, they're seasonal by definition, offering intense nutritional value. A serving is spooned into a bowl, the vegetables are eaten with chopsticks but there's no spoon, so villagers drink the broth from the bowl. If zucchini is in season, the flowers are added in (a bit later, of course); and if pumpkin is in season, the leaves are added in (a bit later, of course). If you're making something with leek and potato, then the leek is added in (a bit later, of course). And the size of the pieces makes no difference. In the absence of chopping boards, potatoes are peeled by knife in the hand, and then roughly cut into pieces in the hand too. There's no regular stirring, or mashing, so the result is entirely rustic.

The process is not dissimilar for basic fish soup. The same amount of water, a little tomato, and some chilli and salt (wow!).

Spicy Dai Tomato Soup

This delicious but very spicy Dai soup traditionally incorporates slices of a cake made with green beans. This may not be easy to find (or make!) so here slices of rice cake are substituted. If you don't have access to rice cake either, use about 25 g/1 oz wide flat dried rice noodles. Blanch first and then add to the soup.

INGREDIENTS

200 g / 7 oz rice cake, sliced
4 tomatoes, cut into chunks
12 chillies, halved lengthwise
4 cloves garlic, finely crushed
1 tbsp Sichuan peppercorns
1 tsp salt • 20 g / ¾ oz coriander sprigs
20 g / ¾ oz mint sprigs, roughly chopped
2 tbsp Chinese black vinegar
1 tbsp soy sauce
225 ml / 8 fl oz hot water
2 spring onions, for garnish • 2 sprigs coriander, for garnish
1 tbsp oil, for frying

METHOD

1. Heat oil in a pan and stir-fry chillies, garlic and peppercorns until aromatic
2. Add tomatoes and press the pieces into the pan to fuse flavours. Add salt
3. Simmer until the tomatoes have reduced to a thick sauce
4. Add coriander, mint, vinegar and soy sauce and simmer for 1 minute
5. Add water and simmer for 20 minutes
6. Add rice cake slices and cook for about 3 minutes until al dente. Garnish and serve hot or cold

Bai Chicken Soup

This dish is an excellent example of the sour-spicy combination which is at the heart of Bai cooking. If you are unable to find quince, substitute with 100 g / 3½ oz green mango and 225 g / 8 oz tamarind pulp. This recipe comes from Zhang Li Fen, originally from Kunming, but now living in Dali where she works as a government chef.

INGREDIENTS

1 chicken, cut into bite-sized pieces (about 1 kilo), skin on and bone in
30 g / 1 oz Yunnan ham, finely sliced
10 Sichuan peppers
1 quince, thinly sliced
5 cm / 2 in piece ginger, crushed
2 tsp salt
Packet preserved green chillies

METHOD

1. Soak chicken pieces in cold water to remove any blood
2. In a pan, cover chicken with cold water and bring to the boil. Skim
3. Add ham slices, Sichuan peppers, quince and ginger. Bring back to the boil and remove any foam. Add salt
4. Lower heat and simmer for 15 minutes
5. Add 1 tbsp of liquid from the preserved chillies, plus 5 or 6 chillies
6. Continue simmering for about 30 minutes until the chicken is cooked through

Pork Rib & Radish Soup

The long, slow cooking method results in a richly flavoured soup. The water chestnuts bring a sense of sweetness, and the Sichuan peppercorns a bit of a kick.

INGREDIENTS

300 g / 10½ oz pork rib, cut into chunks
300 g / 10½ oz green radish (or similar)
2 water chestnuts, halved
2 thick slices ginger
1 piece star anise
1 tsp Sichuan peppercorns
Pinch of salt

METHOD

1. Put the pork, chestnuts, ginger, star anise and peppercorns in a clay pot and cover with water. Bring to the boil, reduce heat, cover, and simmer for 1 hour until the liquid is reduced by about a third
2. Slice the radish into chunky wheels, and then cut those in crescent shapes. Add to the pot with a pinch of salt, bring back to the boil, cover, and simmer for 1 hour

Sour-Spicy Fish & Tomato Soup in Clay Pot

The Dai have ready access to sour tomatoes for this traditional dish. If the tomatoes being used are not sour, ameliorate with 1 or 2 tbsp Chinese black vinegar. Usually, a small whole fish would be used: it's up to you if you want to fiddle with the bones. The fish chosen should have a meaty texture with a bite to it. The chilli paste can be store-bought, or made at home (see page 20). Similarly, preserved vegetables can be store-bought or made at home (see page 18). Adjust the amount of chillies to taste.

INGREDIENTS

300 g / 10½ oz fish fillet (e.g. green carp) or 2 small whole fish, washed and dried
3 thin slices ginger
2 spring onions, white part only, finely chopped
2 tsp Sichuan peppercorns
1 tsp chilli paste / chilli chutney
100 g / 3½ oz tofu, cut into thick slices
1 green tomatoes, half cut into quarters and half into slices
500-750 ml / 1-1½ pints water, depending on size of pot
1 tsp salt • 2 tsp oil, for frying
2 sprigs coriander, for garnish

METHOD

1. Heat the oil in a clay pot, and stir in ginger, spring onion, peppercorns and chilli paste
2. Add tomato chunks (and vinegar, if using) and squash the pieces into the oil until broken down
3. Add water and salt, and bring to the boil. Place fish in the pot, cover, bring the heat down, and simmer for 15 minutes
4. Add tofu and tomato slices, bring back to the boil, top with coriander, and serve

Pork Broth with Yunnan Ham

Get a clay pot for cooking dishes such as this! This clean-flavoured, greenish-coloured broth with thin strands of ham is fresh and healthy.

INGREDIENTS

1 small radish (about 20 cm / 8 in long and 8 cm / 3 in diameter)
1 litre / 4 pints pork stock
25 g / 1 oz Yunnan ham (discarded, dry off-cuts), cut into four chunks
25 g / 1 oz ginger, julienned
A few slices of good quality lean ham, julienned

METHOD

1. Slice the radish into bite-sized pieces
2. Put stock in a pan with the end part of the ham, radish and ginger, and bring to the boil. Simmer for 15 minutes
3. Remove ginger. Add the lean ham. Cook for one minute, then turn heat off

Village Vegetable Soup

This is a little more modern, rather more sophisticated soup than the typical village offering, yet still using vegetables from the typical kitchen garden. The vegetables can be forked through for a more fused flavour, and augmented with a herb such as sage. The soup can also be blended until smooth.

INGREDIENTS

1 kilo / 2¼ pounds potatoes, peeled and roughly chopped
450 g / 1 lb pumpkin, peeled and roughly chopped
2 leeks, cleaned and cut into chunks
1 bunch spinach, roughly chopped
1½ tsp salt
1 litre / 2 pints water

METHOD

1. Place potatoes, pumpkin and leek in a large pot, add salt, and cover with water. Bring to the boil and simmer for about half an hour until the vegetables are tender
2. Add spinach and simmer for a further 3 minutes

Chicken & Foraged Mushroom Soup

The best, actually only, chicken for this dish is the black-skinned chicken which may have bronze-coloured or white feathers. This chicken does not supply much meat, but the meat it does is so flavoursome because it comes straight from the bone. The black chicken has very yellow fat and, in Kunming, chickens are bred so that people can utilise that fat. Put in a pan and fried, it releases its oil, which is traditionally used to fry vegetables with ginger and garlic.

INGREDIENTS

1 black-skinned chicken
200 g / 7 oz fresh mushrooms or 150 g / 5 oz dried mushrooms
or use a combination of 100 g / 3½ oz fresh mushrooms and 100 g / 3½ oz dried mushrooms

METHOD

For the chicken:

1. Clean the chicken, cut breast and back meat away from carcass. Set this meat aside to use in another dish. Finely chop everything from head to tail, from wing to thigh into about 1 cm x 1 cm / ½ in x ½ in pieces. Rinse
2. Bring a pot of water to the boil and blanch chicken in it. Remove chicken, set aside, and throw away the water
3. Fill a second pot with water, throw in the chicken pieces, bring to the boil, turn the heat down, cover, and simmer for 4 hours without skimming

For the mushrooms:

1. If using fresh mushrooms, brush clean and then finely slice
2. If using dried mushrooms, soak overnight in warm water

To complete the soup:

1. For fresh mushrooms, add them to the soup (after the 4 hours' cooking time) and cook for 3 minutes
2. If using dried mushrooms, add to the chicken broth and simmer for another hour
3. If using a combination, throw in dried mushrooms after the broth has cooked for 4 hours and, one hour later, throw in fresh mushrooms and cook for 3 minutes

The Flower Festival

JUNE 21-23: Torrential rain and the loudest, most vivid of thunderstorms overnight have left the roads flooded and the central market sodden. But everyone has risen early, nonetheless. The shoe-shine boys on the periphery have their work cut out for them as shoppers' footwear becomes encrusted with the yellow mud. But there's no option for a lie-in. Everyone is there buying what's needed for a special lunch, as today is the city of Yiliang's annual Flower Festival. Or at least the culmination of a festival which began two days before, with avenues of stalls set up showing hundreds of different flowers, decorative plants, trees and fruit-bearing bushes; from exquisite orchids and the palest of pink roses to ugly Venus fly-catchers and sweet-smelling osmanthus plants.

Breakfast market vendors go about their usual business, serving meals of deep-fried dough sticks, the sticks expertly twisted in the oil, with a thick soy-bean milk custard. There are the typical bowls of rice noodles, and also stews of goat and dog, the carcasses of which hang close by. But elsewhere the place is heaving with shoppers out buying traditional foods for the day. It is busier than even during the Lunar New Year.

Lunch in fact is a rather a simple meal in the same way that festival food often is: a deliberate show of frugality for the purpose of ushering in an era of plenty. The Flower Festival coincides with the Dragon Boat Festival, but in this city the event is about far more than the racing and the accompanying *zongzi* stuffed leaves which recall the legend of the poet Qu Yuan. Here, in a province famous for its flowers – and this city is a particular centre for them – there's a strong sense of letting the bad things "go" and letting in the good. Children wear brightly coloured little cotton bracelets (like simple friendship bands), woven on street corners, to ward off the devil, and outside every house some special green branches hang by the door for the same purpose.

Zongzi are served, of course, but here they're simply plain steamed glutinous rice stuffed in reed leaves, the rice taking its flavours and aromas from the leaf as the parcels steam. A sprinkle of sugar is the only (optional) adornment once the sticky leaves have been pulled away to reveal the rice. Then there's a bowl of long, thin, round rice noodles, bought hand-made in the market, over which is poured a simple chicken broth. Toppings are preserved cabbage, chopped spring onion, a ground meat preparation, finely chopped chilli, and perhaps a piece of stewed chicken. After that, diners tuck into whole steamed heads of garlic,

steamed beans from which the shell must be removed before eating (similar to broad beans but larger), plain steamed breads and hard-boiled eggs. Each of these is eaten by itself, with not even a nod in the direction of the chilli jam. There's not said to be much direct symbolism except perhaps that the chicken broth can stain fingers red – and thus ward off the devil – and that egg shells used to be stained red for the same reason. Though red, of course, is also the Chinese colour for luck.

By late afternoon, although the street fair is still in full swing, village families are beginning to make tracks, the children having played at the fairground while the parents enjoyed snacks from Sichuan or Hunan provinces, or purchased jade from a Myanmar booth or candies from a Thai one. Every family has purchased a plant to bring home. Groups of friends are gathering downtown to drink tea and play mahjong. There's a distinct holiday feeling in the air.

Some way out of the city, this family travels to Grandfather Li's home for dinner. He's the former chief of his village, and his cooking skills are such that he used to cook for village wedding parties. Grandfather Li lives in a house which he built 40 years ago, around a central yard, and here he keeps pigs and chickens, and grows a few herbs (like mint) and vegetables (such as peppers) in rough boxes. At Spring Festival, he'll always slaughter a pig, but today he has slaughtered a chicken. Tonight's Han dinner is not traditional food for the Flower Festival – because there isn't really anything – but it is a typical village dinner, and tonight he has three tables to cook for.

A few guests are chatting, seated on little stools, with the sounds of barking and cock-a-doodle-doing behind them. One woman is setting to on a pile of preserved vegetables with a cleaver, another is cleaning mint, spring onions, coriander and Chinese chives under running water in the courtyard, ready to be chopped by another female. Mise-en-place is a female occupation on these kinds of festive nights. Cooking is for the men. (On an ordinary night, the women would do the cooking).

The kitchen boasts original quaint shelves and cupboards, its centrepiece being a wood (and pine cone)-fired oven with a huge wok nestling there. Check the bucket of clean water inside the door, a bucket for slops just outside the door, and a rack bearing various pots and baskets and ladles – and that's about it. There's a red plastic bag hanging from a hook, from which the heads of two roast ducks slump out. The famous "toasted" duck of this area, they'll be chopped up into two-bite-size pieces later.

There's a lot going on around Grandfather Li but he seems to have everything under control. A pot of pork belly and chunks of raw pumpkin lurks on the ground just outside the kitchen door, but mutton with potatoes is the first dish cooking in the wok. That is quickly transferred to a serving bowl while Head Chef splashes some water into the wok and wipes it over with a bamboo brush (into the slops that water goes). There are some mod cons – a microwave and a couple of electric rings. A son-in-law places a pan of large eggplant chunks in water on one of those rings. Thunder rolls and the rain greedily follows, so the outdoor chairs and tables are rapidly moved to an area under cover and a living room. A tabby cat sullenly jumps off the traditionally tiled roof, seeking shelter.

Vegetable oil is poured into the wok and in goes the contents of a pink plastic bag: eel pieces. Old, almost grey ginger, sliced into small coins is next, and then slabs of pork belly and the pumpkin chunks from the waiting pot are tipped into the wok. Then, spoons of the thick Yunnan chilli jam, made with – among other things – soy bean powder, ground *huajiao*, black cardamom powder and chilli powder.

The fire's gone down a bit so Grandfather is stoking it, sitting on a little stool as he does so, an image of the kitchen god on the wall above his head. Then in go mint leaves, the top part of the Chinese leek, chopped garlic – and we are done. It is transferred to a series of serving dishes which are speedily dispatched. The cooking of the next dish has already begun.

And so it goes, in long-rehearsed movements, until the twelfth and final dish, fish in a spicy gravy with mint leaves, is simmering – and guests are asked to please start eating. There's been (at least) one classic moment, when a grandson asks Grandfather to please use less MSG... though comments are heard that even Grandfather would never consider using MSG in Yunnan foraged mushroom dishes. Grandfather finally sits down with a stiff drink, smiles and clinks cheers, then prods about in a couple of dishes with his chopsticks. He ponders: had perhaps there been one table rather than three, the food could have been that much better? □

EGGS

Eggs are hugely popular in Yunnan, more so probably than the chicken that laid them. From scrambled and steamed to fried or preserved, dishes can be as simple as eggs fried with tomato and spring onion (the best, richer one is made with lard) to frittata or omelette exotically made with rose petals.

Laid by chickens invariably fed on corn and rice (as opposed to scraps), eggs here are delicious, the yolks deep yellow in colour. The quail egg famously shows up in Cross the Bridge Noodles, where it poaches in the steaming broth.

Egg and Tomato Bake

This is a modern take on a very popular dish traditionally served with rice – and almost resembles a quiche. For this, you need an 18 cm / 7 in pan with deep sides and an oven-proof metal handle.

INGREDIENTS

4 eggs, beaten until fluffy
3 ripe tomatoes, cut into large chunks
1 small red onion, cut into small chunks
1 leek or celery stick, cut into small pieces
1 bunch flowering garlic chives (about 200 g / 7 oz), cut into 1 cm / ½ in lengths, reserving the flowers
175 g / 6 oz self-raising flour • Generous 50 ml / 1¾ fl oz water
1 tsp Sichuan peppercorns
2 tsp chilli flakes • Salt and pepper
Water, as necessary • Oil, for frying

METHOD

1. Heat 1 tsp oil in a frying pan, and stir-fry onion and leek (or celery) until translucent
2. Add tomatoes, Sichuan peppercorns, 1 tsp chilli flakes and ½ tsp salt and cook for 3-5 minutes until the tomatoes are tender. Add water as necessary
3. Add chive stalks, stir to combine, and set aside to cool
4. Combine flour and water, and then gradually add the eggs with some salt and pepper
5. Meanwhile, pre-heat the oven to 180°C (350°F)
6. Heat 1 tbsp oil in the oven-proof pan over a medium heat and pour in the egg mixture
7. Top with the tomato mixture, and sprinkle with the flowers and remaining chilli flakes. Reduce the flame and allow the egg to brown a little
8. Place in a heated oven and bake for 5-10 minutes until the egg is just set

Fried Tomato with Egg

This is a ubiquitous traditional village dish but, because it's so simple, it must be made with the best (organic) tomatoes and eggs. It can also be made with spring melon.

INGREDIENTS

2 eggs, beaten with 1 tsp salt

2 medium tomatoes, each cut into 8 pieces

Salt and pepper, to taste

Oil, for frying

METHOD

1. Heat a little oil in a wok, and roughly scramble the eggs by swirling into clumps. Remove and set aside
2. Add a little more oil, and stir-fry the tomatoes. Add a little salt and pepper and, when the tomatoes are slightly caramelised and soft, stir in eggs and serve immediately

If using spring melon:

Thinly slice the melon, then proceed in the manner as above, frying melon until tender in place of the tomatoes.

Scrambled Egg with Spicy Pork

Everyone loves it! Instead of making scrambled eggs, a second option is to fry the egg until brown and crispy, then chop up this crepe with a spatula and stir in the pork.

INGREDIENTS

300 g / 10½ oz pork loin, sliced very finely
1 tsp soy sauce
2 tsp chilli flakes
4 eggs, beaten
2 spring onions, finely chopped
1 tsp oil, for frying

METHOD

1. Marinate the pork with soy and chilli for 10 minutes
2. Heat 1 tsp of oil in a wok, and fry the pork. Push meat to one side
3. Pour in beaten egg and scramble until it begins to set
4. Combine with pork, add spring onions, and cook for 1 minute

Steamed Egg with Preserved Vegetables

INGREDIENTS

100 g / 3½ oz preserved vegetables, drained and chopped
2 tsp chilli flakes
4 eggs
50 ml / 2 fl oz water
1 tsp sesame oil
Salt and pepper, to taste
Yunnan ham fat, for frying

METHOD

1. Heat pan and fry ham fat, preserved vegetables and chilli flakes until aromatic. Place in a bowl ready for steaming
2. Beat eggs well and gradually add water. Beat in sesame oil, salt and pepper
3. Pour egg mixture over the preserved vegetables, and place dish in a steamer. Steam for 7 minutes and serve piping hot

Egg Rolls

These stuffed egg crepes are sour and spicy but in a delicate way with the combination of pickles, garlic chives and bean sprouts. Ramp them up with a tomato salsa (see page 24) if desired. The recipe is inspired by the increasing sophistication of menus in Kunming, with international chefs being hired to serve an increasingly high-end clientele in smaller cities such as Jinghong, too.

INGREDIENTS

4 eggs, beaten until fluffy with ½ tsp salt
100 g / 3½ oz flowering garlic chives, cut into 2.5 cm / 1 in lengths
50 g / 1¾ oz bean sprouts
225 g / 8 oz pickled radish and carrots (see page 19)
1 tsp chilli flakes
1 tsp salt
Oil, for frying

METHOD

1. Brush 1 tsp oil over a flat pan. When hot, add half the egg mixture and swirl it quickly across the pan to make the crepe. Once browned, flip to the other side and brown. Remove and set aside
2. In a hot pan, quickly fry the garlic chives with chilli flakes and ½ tsp salt. Add bean sprouts and pickles and toss until well combined
3. Assemble this filling on to the lower part of the crepe, bring sides together, then roll as tightly as possible

Steamed Egg with Shiitake Mushrooms

The key ingredient here is the egg, and the perfect, light texture which is achieved through steaming. Across the world, people fine-tune egg cooking to time but also to personal taste – soft or hard boiled; soft or hard scrambled; poached versus fried. There is also an art to steaming, depending on the size of the dish, the shape of the double boiler, and even the altitude of your stove. Experiment with this very simple dish!

INGREDIENTS

4 dried shiitake, soaked for at least 4 hours until very tender
½ tbsp preserved vegetables
4 eggs
Scant 125 ml / 4½ fl oz cooled water
Salt, to taste

METHOD

1. Drain the shiitake, slice very finely, and combine with the preserved vegetables. Place in a steaming dish
2. Lightly beat the eggs and mix in water and salt, beating until the texture is smooth
3. Pour egg mixture over the mushrooms and preserved vegetables, and steam for 3 minutes

Bitter Melon & Celery Omelette

INGREDIENTS

100 g / 3½ oz wood ear mushrooms, sliced

1 small bitter melon, cut in half and then finely sliced

½ stick celery, sliced into pieces the same size as the melon

4 large dried chillies, chopped

3 eggs

Salt and pepper, to taste

Oil, for frying

METHOD

1. Heat some oil in a pan and stir-fry mushrooms with chillies and salt and pepper for about 1 minute
2. Add bitter melon and celery, cook for a further minute
3. Move these ingredients to the side of the pan and add a little more oil to the pan
4. Beat the eggs with a little salt and pepper, then combine all the ingredients
5. Heat oil in a pan, and cook in two batches

Lunch in a Dai Village

Long black hair is swept off her face and into a discreet bun. Orchid clears a table and elegantly sweeps the leaves off the café terrace onto the pavement. Someone's having an espresso, another a glass of Chilean white wine. Four Chinese men, all smoking, sit down at one of the outdoor tables, and out comes an order pad. Three fruit juices and one lime soda. She empties the ash tray. Appropriately lazy jazz refrains waft out from the café's bar. It's a typically warm and lazy afternoon in Jinghong: in about half an hour, at 3pm, the banks and offices will re-open. Jinghong is siesta city. Everywhere else, banks re-open at 2pm.

Orchid, on the other hand, works very hard. She shares work with the waiting staff but in fact she personally opened Mei Mei Café, now amazingly located on the city's main drag, Menglong Street, in 2000, and it is a very good business. But Orchid (family name Zhang), not yet 40 years of age, is not sure if she wants this kind of – business – life. The money is great, but the business has taken over her life. To find the staff, to stay consistent, to keep everyone happy, is no easy task. Consistency of product is not easy, either. Keeping a "western" café – which also sells Chinese and local food – means you have to have a certain quality of steak, for example. But sellers here are unscrupulous and, at greater price, she buys from a Muslim butcher because at least she knows there's integrity there.

She has already bought a piece of land in the countryside, surrounded by paddy fields, and will build a house there and perhaps open a small café with a couple of guest rooms above. She will hire local village girls to help her. She's bought the land about 20 km outside Dali, somewhat north of Jinghong, because that's where she's from.

Orchid, a thoughtful woman with expressive eyes and a big but meaningful smile, is of the Bai ethnic minority, but runs a business in a Dai city. Today, she's hosting a lunch in a restaurant in the Dai village of Manhunshuo, a now-prosperous village which turned around its fortunes by gaining a reputation among tourists for cooking some of the best Dai food around. It's a peaceful place, with mountains in the distance whichever way you look.

Before Yunnan province was born, the region was a Dai kingdom, and this village was tasked (every village had a different function) with no less than cooking for the king. The reverence for the cuisine, and the know-how, have never gone away.

The lunch is a "set" – a pre-ordered selection of some 15 dishes, plus two kinds of rice: plain glutinous rice, and pineapple rice. There are three dips (tomato salsa, a herby sour green one, and another one of peanuts, quite thin in texture), and little dishes of chilli flakes. Slightly scraggy-looking fried pork belly, pork ribs and chicken wings are served in little baskets, on banana leaves. The lemongrass-scented fish is sublime.

There's a platter of seasonal fresh bamboo shoots – tender and bitter, as they should be – and baby corns; and another of cucumber strips and two kinds of local herbs (English names unknown). Of the two soups, one contains the leaves of a local tree, there's a plate of a variety of edible ferns unseen outside this region, and a plate of something in the black moss family growing in the river water, which is first dried, and ends up tasting a bit like grass – it is fabulously unusual. A delicious omelette is coloured murky green by a plant known locally as "stinky vegetable" – English name unknown.

Orchid is really keen on the Dai cuisine. The use of every kind of herb and vegetable, the lightness of the food, the lack of frying, the sour sauces. No one here, she comments, is overweight. Given the higher altitude of her home city, and the cooler weather, the food tends to be richer and more oily, she says, and there's

lots of milk and cheese – to which she is somewhat intolerant. And she likes Dai people. While her own people might be more reserved, though she cites the Naxi as being the most private, she appreciates the Dai openness to outsiders. That culture is reflected in her own restaurant, where her chef is Akha and her staff are Bulang, Akha and Jinuo. They're honest and hardworking, she says, and they all get along together. One of her neighbouring restaurants is Muslim, and the Hui owner is a good friend of hers.

But she's getting rather frustrated with some of her clientele. "Chinese people have to learn to respect," she says. "This is something missing in this country. If you travel around the world, you will realise you have to respect." She is planning a small tent card for each table detailing what her standards are. No spitting, no bringing your own food, no leaving of litter, no loud voices. And, if you want better service, please respect the closing hours. She says that just yesterday she reprimanded a customer for summoning staff in a rude way, but the guest took it very well. "They just don't know," she says.

She's not sure of the future of Jinghong. Already, where tourists might have hung out for a few days at Mei Mei Café, they now move in and then swiftly out, enjoying less and less the atmosphere of what is emerging as a significant city. And what of Dali? Dali, she says, with its Old City and traditional architecture, is already full of culture. And, increasingly, people like musicians and artists are moving there: "interesting people" who "want to live their own life." In Dali, she says, "everyone is different from each other."

Back at her café, when the early evening rush is waning, she sits down for a glass or two of red wine (from France), and will then return to the downtown home she shares with her Belgian husband. □

Growing Grapes in Yunnan

Grapes with names as evocative as Rose Honey, Crystal and French Wild grow in some of the most beautiful parts of Yunnan Province. Shan Shumin, the softly-spoken general manager of Yunnan Red, the province's largest wine producer, is hosting a tasting at the company's winery in Mi Le, not far from Kunming.

From the tasting room's terrace, there are sweeping views over hundreds of hectares of vineyards, dotted with little white houses. The typical hilly terrain renders the vistas as charming as any in European wine country, and there's even a red-roofed church down the slope. The backdrop, though, is all Yunnan: dark, brooding mountains.

All China attention in the international wine community seems to be on the northern provinces of Shandong and Ningxia, so is Yunnan really suited to grape cultivation?

"If you choose the right grapes, it is suitable," Shan says, citing in particular the red grapes Rose Honey and French Wild, and the white grape Crystal. "These grapes have adapted themselves well to the altitude and climate, and they do not use so much water." At around 1,400-1,800 metres, the region has the highest elevations of all China's vineyards – and along with those in Argentina, are among the world's highest. These high altitudes, and the clean dry air, provide resistance to insects and disease, negating the use of pesticides and sprays. The vineyards are close to the Tropic of Cancer, meaning that temperatures plummet compared with daytime highs: climatic conditions vines tend to flourish in.

Research seems somewhat patchy, but it is believed that vines were first planted two centuries ago in Shangri-La by French missionaries. It is mooted, further, that "overseas" Chinese may have brought cuttings back from Vietnam. Also, it is thought that the main varieties such as French Wild and Rose Honey (the latter so-called because it smells like roses and honey, both of which are strongly associated with Yunnan) were grapes from France subsequently destroyed by the phylloxera outbreak which decimated many of the vineyards of Europe in the late 19th century. Yunnan may be the only place where they are growing now.

Certainly Rose Honey makes very attractive, scented wine; and apparently the lifted aromas of the white grape Crystal (which can also be consumed as a table grape) emanate from the vineyard during harvesting. The finished wine smells of all the tropical fruits which grow so beautifully in southern Yunnan, but it has a lovely acidity and even a mineral edge. French Wild appears to have similarities with Cabernet Franc and Cabernet Sauvignon – deeper and more vegetal than the Rose Honey.

Today, says Shan, the domestic consumer can afford to buy wine – but lacks knowledge. "They think only French wine is good. They don't realise that local wine has two levels of quality." The local wine industry got off to a bad start, he says, with wine actually being half wine and half water. And grape growers need to remember to limit yields, and improve on, for example, trellising techniques.

Since the 1990s, quality has been steadily rising, and there's money to be made from growing grapes to sell to wineries. "Now, some wineries such as Grace [in Shanxi Province] get international awards," says Shan. "It will take time for other wineries to catch up, though." □

MUSHROOMS

The atmosphere in Yunnan's city wet markets when foraged mushroom season is in full swing is electric. Of course there's money to be made, and that creates a buzz. The most expensive mushroom, the ill-formed, grey-and-white *gan ba jung*, is this month going for 1,300 yuan a kilo. This summer's season has started late (usually there's something in June) but with the relentless rain now, in late July, the baskets are aplenty. Not that this necessarily means that prices will be lower. Customers, and vendors, pore over varieties in shades of green, yellow, blue orange and even dark pink, not to mention every nuance of brown. The season can run as late as November, but the mushrooms are very cheap by then.

Ask people of Yunnan about their favourite food, and many will highlight mushrooms above indigenous lake fish or Yunnan ham. Mostly the cooking is very simple, to retain the all-important aroma, flavour and, perhaps most importantly, texture. Rarely is anything beyond garlic, spring onion, local green peppers and some chilli put into the mix.

Cultivated mushrooms are available all year round, as are dried mushrooms, but there's nothing quite like the mushrooms picked early in the morning, in the rain, and carried down the mountain to the domestic kitchen, the restaurant, or the local market.

Bamboo Shoots with Shiitake and Wood Ear Mushrooms

This dish is very traditional in the south of Yunnan since bamboo is widely grown across Xishuangbanna; and wood ear mushrooms can even be bought from the market ready-soaked. It is all about texture: the crunch of the wood ear and the fresh tenderness of the bamboo. Since fresh bamboo is rarely available outside Yunnan and other parts of the region, here canned shoots are substituted.

INGREDIENTS

1 can bamboo shoots
4 dried shiitake mushrooms, soaked overnight
1 handful dried wood ear mushrooms, soaked overnight
2 chillies, finely chopped
3 spring onions, cut into 3 cm / 1 in pieces (keep white and green parts separate)
1 tsp salt
1 tsp pepper
Oil, for frying

METHOD

1. Drain the mushrooms and set the water aside. Slice the shiitake. Cut the wood ear into bite-sized pieces (as necessary)
2. Drain the bamboo shoots. Cut into about the same thickness as the shiitake, but about twice the width
3. Heat 1 tsp oil in a pan and fry the shiitake with the white part of the spring onion, chilli and a little salt
4. Add shoots with 2 tbsp of the mushroom soaking water and fuse for 1 minute
5. Add wood ears and some pepper, cover, and braise for 2-5 minutes (depending on the shoots, and it may be necessary to add a little more mushroom soaking water)
6. Stir in the green part of the spring onion and serve immediately

Enoki Mushrooms with Spicy Soy Bean Paste

Enoki are the (Japanese) mushrooms, light beige in colour with long and skinny stems, all growing out of a single thick root (which is unsuitable for eating). They are popularly used in hotpots, such as sukiyaki, or lightly blanched for salads. Here, they are given the spicy sauce treatment. The large enoki stem (some 3 cm / 1 in thick) is becoming more and more popular.

INGREDIENTS

300 g / 10½ oz enoki mushrooms
150 g / 5½ oz enoki stem
1½ tbsp chilli paste
1 tsp black bean paste
2 cloves garlic, finely sliced
2 shallots, finely sliced
100 g / 3½ oz mustard greens, chopped into bite-sized pieces
1 red pepper, cut into bite-sized pieces
1 tsp chilli flakes • Salt, to taste • Oil, for frying

METHOD

1. Remove the mushroom base from the enoki bunch and cut the bunch into two parts vertically. Cut the stem into thin slices horizontally
2. Heat a little oil in a pan, turn the heat down, and fry the enoki with the chilli paste and black bean paste. Set aside
3. Heat a little more oil and stir-fry garlic and shallots, then toss in mustard greens and red pepper. Stir-fry for 3 minutes with the chilli flakes
4. Push to one side of the pan, then fry the mushrooms for a further minute
5. Arrange vegetables on a plate and top with the mushrooms

Yunnan Ham with Autumn Melon & Shiitake Mushrooms

INGREDIENTS

10 g / ½ oz Yunnan ham

6 shiitake mushrooms, soaked overnight in 450 ml / 1 pint hot water, then halved, soaking water reserved

1 autumn melon, peeled and thinly sliced

2 slices of ginger, cut into slivers

1 tsp salt

Oil, for frying

METHOD

1. Thinly slice the ham into about the same size as the mushroom halves
2. Heat a little oil in a wok and stir-fry ham and mushrooms for 2 minutes. Add 1 tbsp of mushroom soaking water to fuse flavours. Remove from pan and set aside
3. Add another tsp of oil to the wok, and stir in melon, ginger and salt and stir-fry for 2 minutes. Add the remainder of the mushroom soaking water, cover, and steam until tender
4. Return ham and mushrooms to the pan, and stir together for 1 minute

Porcini Mushrooms with Yunnan Ham & Green Chilli Peppers

This is the classic Yunnan way to prepare foraged mushrooms in season. Large amounts of garlic are traditionally used as, it is said, the garlic turns black in the pan if the mushrooms are poisonous. Many different kinds of mushrooms can be used. In the absence of the likes of porcini, use steak or Portobello mushrooms. If you are not using Yunnan ham, throw in a tbsp of Parma ham pieces at the end of the cooking process. Yunnan green long chillies are half-spicy, and should be easy to find.

INGREDIENTS

200 g / 7 oz porcini, soaked and sliced
2 green chilli peppers, cut across into 1 cm / ½ in pieces
2 cloves garlic, halved
2 chillies, halved lengthwise
½ tsp salt
Few slices Yunnan ham
3 tbsp oil, for frying

METHOD

1. Heat the oil in a pan and add green peppers, garlic, chillies and salt. Stir-fry for 1 minute
2. Add mushrooms, then ham, and stir for 2 minutes

Stir-Fried Mushrooms with Asparagus Tips

Here, the mushrooms absorb the garlic-infused oil, and the use of pepper balances out the chestnut and mushroom flavours.

INGREDIENTS

75 g / 2¾ oz mushrooms
2-3 cloves garlic, finely sliced
75 g / 2¾ oz asparagus stalks, sliced diagonally (reserve tips)
5 water chestnuts, finely sliced
1 tsp freshly ground black pepper
Salt, to taste
Splash of water
1 tbsp oil, for frying

METHOD

1. Heat oil in a pan and stir in mushrooms and garlic, cook for 2 minutes over a medium heat
2. Add asparagus and bring up the heat, stir-fry for 1 minute
3. Add water chestnuts with a pinch of salt and pepper, and a splash of water, and cook for 2 minutes
4. Sprinkle remaining black pepper on top

Spicy Aromatic Mushrooms

This traditional village dish uses whichever mushrooms are in season.

INGREDIENTS

250 g / 9 oz mixed fresh mushrooms, cleaned with a light brush then roughly sliced
2 tsp chilli flakes
1 tsp freshly ground Sichuan peppercorns
1 tsp salt
2 cloves garlic, sliced
200 g / 7 oz garlic chives, cut into 3 cm / 1 in pieces
1 tsp oil, for frying

METHOD

1. Heat 1 tsp oil in a pan and stir in chilli flakes and Sichuan peppercorns
2. Stir in salt and garlic
3. Add the mushrooms and garlic chives and stir-fry very quickly until tender. This will only take 2 minutes if they are really fresh. Add more oil if necessary (but not water)

Spicy Tofu with Fresh Mushrooms

INGREDIENTS

200 g / 7 oz firm tofu, cut into pieces 5 cm x 3 cm x 1 cm / 2 in x 1 in x ½ in thick
100 g / 3½ oz fresh mushrooms, cleaned and thickly sliced
2 cloves garlic, crushed
1½ tsp Sichuan peppercorns, freshly ground
1½ tsp chilli flakes
1½ tsp salt
Oil, for frying

METHOD

1. In a dry pan, roast peppercorns, chilli flakes and salt together over a gentle flame until aromatic. Set aside
2. Heat 1 tbsp oil in a pan, and lightly pan-fry tofu on two sides. Plate, and sprinkle with the spicy salt
3. Add a little more oil to the pan and fry mushrooms and garlic over a high heat (to avoid water coming out)
4. Top tofu with mushrooms, serve immediately

Mixed Mushrooms with Mustard Greens

Preserved mustard greens are widely used to complement many meat dishes. Here, they are combined with fresh mustard greens to highlight the freshness of the green vegetable and the earthiness of the mushrooms.

INGREDIENTS

6 portobello mushrooms, halved
6 porcini, soaked overnight in 225 ml / 8 fl oz warm water
1 large enoki stem, cut into slices, then halve the slices
1 tbsp preserved mustard greens, leaf part only
1 tsp chilli paste • 3 slices ginger
1 bunch mustard greens, stems only (use the leaves for another dish), washed and dried, sliced into thin strips
1 tsp oil, for frying

METHOD

1. Heat the oil in a pan and add mushrooms, preserved greens and chilli paste. Stir-fry for 2 minutes and push aside
2. Add ginger and stems and stir-fry for 2 minutes
3. Bring the mushrooms back to the centre of the pan, mix together, and serve hot

Foraging for Mushrooms

It's a potentially lethal business: first foraging for mushrooms in the mountains, and then embarking on a mushroom banquet. That's what guides are for, to take the danger out.

About an hour outside Yiliang, the destination is a Yi ethnic minority village called Qiyi, with a restaurant named Xiao Wei Xi much beloved by city folk.

The "Xiao" in the restaurant's name is not from this village; she moved here through marriage, and is now the village head. It is because of her that the village has found such prosperity, mainly through tourism – for this marvellous destination restaurant – and also the annual Torch Festival. It turns out that she has actually rented one side of the mountain, leaving her free to collect mushrooms (and to embark on foraging in general), and thereby cook the most amazing fresh produce available. She also has access to local corn-fed organic chicken and the most remarkable pork.

Today, however, word is out that nothing is to be picked because of some kind of quota. Had it rained more in April and May, there would be more mushrooms to find in June. So whatever is found needs to be left where it is. Wild vegetables and edible ferns may be picked, however.

The guide, in colourful sneakers, leads the way to the mountain. The walk starts on a concrete pathway. We pass a large barbecue, half-obscured in the undergrowth, where every year there's a special dinner, attended only by men, at which a goat is usually cooked. There's a pair of very special trees with deep spiritual significance. This, after all, is the Holy Mountain for the Yi people, and no tree may ever be felled here.

As the path leads into rough terrain, our man in the funky sneakers turns out to be less guide and more goat, barely bothering to monitor the group. It turns out that he is one of the village's few expert mushroom foragers and he casually upturns little piles of pine needles with his foot in his search. Crossing a tiny ditch, he points out the first mushroom of the day, and it happens to be the most expensive of all. It has a slightly ugly black-grey cap with jagged edges, and this week has been selling for 1,300 yuan per kilo in the markets of Yiliang.

There are a couple of small white-capped mushrooms later, but then there's a long stretch with no mushrooms at all. Trekkers are required to hold back stray branches to traverse the sort-of-path which, due to a sprinkling of rain, is becoming a little slippery. After 20 minutes, the route finally becomes flat. And then, there it is, the most beautiful beige-

white mushroom stretching up towards thin rays of sunshine with the lacy edges of its perfect circle.

Something very important is learnt. The most beautiful mushrooms are usually the most poisonous. Case in point: the ugly green ones, of that hue of green assumed by damp metal, which had been plentiful in the morning market, are the most readily available and thus the cheapest. Close to this gorgeous specimen is another almost perfectly formed mushroom, this time with an earth-brown conically shaped cap. Mushrooms grow in ones? Not in harvestable groups? Apparently those ugly green ones do!

A member of the party comments that while foraging last year he had found and harvested four edible mushrooms. But even those four would have been worth 100 yuan in the market. So the group returns necessarily empty-handed, having seen just half a dozen mushrooms, though there was a little patch of edible ferns, now blackening and thus past their best for human consumption. Back at the foot of the mountain are the inevitable bunches of bananas and banana blossoms, nothing exotic or worthy of market prices there, and a tree bearing fuzzy little green fruits – Chinese chestnuts.

Wild food is part of the everyday diet in Yunnan, and foraging for it a normal pursuit. What's growing on one mountainside may differ entirely from what grows on the next, so locals travelling from one city to another sometimes do not even recognise this vegetable here, or that particular fern. Many varieties are given simple, colloquial terms like fish-scale herb, stinky vegetable or wild tomato. But at the very pinnacle of this organic bounty is the Yunnan foraged mushroom, which so dominates the market stall and the restaurant menu in the months of July and August.

Yunnan is famous for mushrooms. There are hundreds of varieties, with names like "monkey head" and "dried beef". There's "chicken oil" (chanterelle), "cow's liver" (porcini) and "sheep stomach" (morels). They grow across the province, and the season tends to be from June to August but can run into November (though by November they are deemed almost worthless). In general they are harvested by farmers or workers dozens of kilometres away from the cities to which they will sell. They will be purchased by a third party who will bring them to market, or they may even be sold from baskets in key tourist spots as if they were apples.

Some get exported – nearby Hong Kong is particularly lucky in this regard – but the best surely stay in the province, because Yunnan people love their mushrooms. They reach prices even higher than the other best-known product, Yunnan ham. Any surplus mushrooms are dried, but locals have little use for these, perhaps sticking them in soup from time to time, but generally preferring to wait for the next season to again enjoy the fresh ones. In any event, the dried ones tend to lack the pungency of, say, Italian dried porcini – yet can still attract high prices, particularly in tourism magnets like Lijiang, and on the Japanese market (Matsutake mushrooms in particular).

Dinnertime approaches. Luckily the crew has earlier found plenty of mushrooms for dinner (quite possibly from another mountain), and the aromas from the large kitchen, complete with two huge woks atop fires fuelled by logs, are as fresh as the forest air. Mushrooms are carefully washed and skilfully chopped, and fat pork is finely sliced.

The restaurant is set around a simple central courtyard; a series of low tables and stools. The view out through the archway is an idyllic vision of gentle tree-lined hills with vegetable terraces at their feet. Diners scatter sunflower seed shells on the floor, and stand on the verandah for a cigarette. It's a long drive out of the city, so not within access of the regular tourist, but the owner is well connected so the place is frequented by the city's leading officials.

The mushroom banquet tonight consists of nine dishes (plus plain boiled rice at the end), three of which feature mushrooms, and three condiments;

though a fourth extra-hot chilli jam arrives later, and this one also features finely sliced mushrooms. The meat dishes are a local "organic" chicken prepared with garlic and star anise in a rich red gravy; and the Yi people's classic boiled pork – slow-cooked in water which is slowly brought to the boil. Finely sliced with fat intact, it is soft and delicious, and all the more so here, since the pork also comes from the local village.

Simple vegetable dishes are potatoes, steamed and roughly chopped, then mixed with spring onions and fire-dried chilli pieces which have been fried in oil. There's steamed leafy green wild vegetable, cooked until soft but not at all slimy. Huge turnips are chopped into chunks and then lightly steamed. Each can be dipped into one of the chilli sauces, but they sing by themselves, grown in such a spot.

The trio of mushroom dishes arrives, with first their extreme aromatic qualities, and then their textures, to appreciate. There's a quiet earthiness to the stir-fried dish; a sweetness to the soup; and a delicacy to the one steamed with spring onion and slices of garlic.

Our host Mr Chen confesses that this is his favourite restaurant (he seems to mean "ever") and certainly it is a no-brainer to pick up on the quality of the produce, even down to the humble but flavourful potatoes. It turns out that the three mushroom dishes, plus the chilli sauce which features mushroom, have all been personally prepared by the owner.

As the thundery skies give way and powder-blue streaks appear between gently drifting clouds, dinner is finishing. But wait, right across from the restaurant, look at those bushes of "torch" fruit – branches of little orange berries little more than the size of a peppercorn. Few know that not only are they edible, as opposed to toxic, but they are delicious; slightly acidic with an almost tannic edge, definitely evocative of (grape) wine. A forager's delight – and the sum total for today. □

VEGETABLES

These dishes are not necessarily vegetarian, but each puts vegetables (or tofu) at centre stage. It's still a hugely popular practice, originating in the need to make a small piece of meat go a long way (finely slice or mince it, and share say one breast of chicken among four or six people), and adding flavour by cooking in animal or poultry fat.

Yunnan is a province which highly prizes its vegetables (indeed, they're a popular export to Hong Kong when something is out of season in Guangdong, or just because they're often better), and not only the wild mushrooms. Wild vegetables and ferns vary across the region, sometimes unique to a particular mountainside, and they are deliciously unusual.

Fried Tofu in Egg Batter

INGREDIENTS

250 g / 9 oz firm tofu, cut into two-bite pieces

2 eggs, beaten with 1 tsp salt

3 sprigs coriander (finely cut the stems and roughly chop the leaves, keep separate)

3 spring onions, finely chopped

Oil, for frying

METHOD

1. Heat 1 tbsp oil in a pan. Dredge tofu pieces in the egg and fry. Place in a warm dish
2. Meanwhile, mix together any leftover egg with the coriander stems and spring onions. Heat another 1 tbsp oil and scramble this mixture until dry. Place on tofu and top with coriander leaves

Celery with Spicy Sliced Chicken

Chinese celery is long, thin and almost white in colour, as compared with the European one which is thicker and green. Remove any fibrous threads and dry ends, in the usual way.

INGREDIENTS

1 chicken breast, finely sliced across the grain
1 tbsp chilli paste
6 stalks Chinese celery, washed and cut into 3 cm / 1 in pieces
½ tsp salt
Oil, for frying

METHOD

1. Mix together chicken and chilli paste
2. Heat 1 tsp oil in a pan and fry chicken until just cooked. Set to one side of the pan
3. In the same pan, adding a little more oil if necessary, fry celery with the salt for a maximum 2 minutes. Stir in chicken, cook for 1 minute and serve

Fresh Soy Beans with Chilli & Star Anise

Other fresh beans such as fava beans or broad beans can be readily substituted.

INGREDIENTS

200 g / 7 oz fresh soy beans
2 tbsp oil
2 dried red chillies, seeds removed and chopped
2 star anise
2 cloves garlic, finely sliced
175 ml / 6 fl oz chicken stock
½ tsp salt

METHOD

1. In a wok, heat oil and stir-fry chillies, garlic and star anise for 2 minutes. Add beans and stock and bring to the boil
2. Cover, lower the heat and simmer until the beans are soft and the liquid has evaporated (depending on the beans, this may take up to 20 minutes). Stir occasionally. Add salt to taste and serve

Fresh Soy Beans with Yunnan Ham

INGREDIENTS

200 g / 7 oz fresh soy beans
2 cloves garlic, finely sliced
100 g / 3½ oz Yunnan ham, cut into 1 cm / ⅓ in squares
175 ml / 6 fl oz chicken stock
½ tsp salt (optional)
1 tbsp oil, for frying

METHOD

1. In a wok, heat oil and fry garlic until browned. Add ham and cook for 2 minutes
2. Stir in beans, and pour in chicken stock. Bring to the boil
3. Cover, reduce heat, and simmer until the beans are soft and the liquid has evaporated

Steamed Pumpkin with Honey

When pumpkin is in season, it is delicious and nutritious, not to mention colourful. This is a dish often chosen for festivals and banquets, but has now become quite trendy in Yunnan's restaurants. Though sweet, it is eaten as a part of the meal and not at the end. Any pumpkin can be used, and cut into any desired shape. Roasting a pumpkin whole locks in the flavours.

Most local honey is derived from rapeseed. Nomadic beekeepers camp out for a month with their hives close to the rapeseed fields. Honeycombs are sold in the markets.

INGREDIENTS

300 g / 10½ oz pumpkin, skinned and cut into 1 cm / ½ in slices
1 tbsp honey

METHOD

1. Arrange the pumpkin slices on a dish and steam for 40 minutes
2. Remove from steamer and drizzle with honey

Asparagus Stems & Broccoli Stalks with Spicy Pork Loin

This traditional Yunnan dish uses only the stalks of asparagus rather than the tips, and the thick stalk of Chinese broccoli rather than the leaves and flowers.

INGREDIENTS

200 g / 7 oz pork loin, finely sliced across the grain
1 tsp chilli paste
1 tsp Sichuan peppercorns
4 thick stalks Chinese broccoli (*gai laan*)
8 asparagus stalks
½ bunch yellow garlic chives
4 dried chillies • ½ tsp salt
50 ml / 1¾ fl oz water • Oil, for frying

METHOD

1. Mix the pork with the chilli paste and peppercorns
2. Peel the vegetable stalks and cut into strips about half the size of a little finger. Cut the chives into the same length
3. Heat 1 tsp oil in a pan and fry the pork for 1 minute. Remove
4. Add a further 1 tsp oil and fry stems with chillies and salt. Add water and continue cooking uncovered until the stalks are tender
5. Stir in pork, to warm through and combine flavours
6. Sprinkle with garlic chives, and serve

If using bamboo shoots:
Shred the shoots as per broccoli and asparagus. Add an extra ½ tsp salt

Zucchini with Sliced Pork & Dried Shrimps

INGREDIENTS

2 small zucchini, sliced into thin wheels

100 g / 3½ oz pork loin, finely sliced against the grain

100 g / 3½ oz dried shrimps, soaked in 100 ml / 3½ fl oz for 2 hours, then drained and dried. Retain soaking water

2 dried chillies

Small knob ginger, sliced in half

2 tsp chilli flakes

Oil, for frying

METHOD

1. Heat 1 tsp oil and stir-fry ginger. Add pork and stir-fry until almost cooked. Remove the pork
2. Add shrimps and chillies, fry until aromatic. Remove
3. Stir in zucchini and the shrimp-soaking water and cook for about 1 minute. If the vegetable is still not soft, cover and continue cooking
4. Add the pork and allow it to braise for 2 minutes
5. Plate, and top with shrimps and chilli flakes

Chinese Broccoli & Asparagus with Breast of Chicken

INGREDIENTS

1 breast chicken, cut into thin strips
1 bunch Chinese broccoli, stalks and flowers only
4 stalks asparagus
1 tsp light soy sauce
1 tsp cornflour
2 cloves garlic, crushed
4 dried chillies
125 ml / 4½ fl oz water
1 tsp salt
Oil, for frying

METHOD

1. Cut broccoli and asparagus into 1 cm / ½ in pieces
2. Toss chicken in the soy sauce. Just before frying, coat with cornflour
3. Heat some oil in a pan and fry the chicken until almost cooked. Set aside
4. Add a little more oil and stir-fry garlic and chilli until aromatic
5. Add the vegetables and stir-fry until the colour is changing to dark green. Add a little salt and the water. Cover and steam for 1 minute. Move vegetables to the side of the pan to make space for the chicken
6. Add the chicken, cook for 2 minutes, then stir everything together

VEGAN

What a bounty of produce (including superfoods spirulina and maca which grow here) and a breadth of dishes there are for the vegan to experience in Yunnan. They're very good at cooking vegetables here: dishes without perhaps much complexity, but remarkable for their true flavours. Florets of cauliflower are steamed with florets of broccoli. Kernels of corn are stir-fried with fresh green peas, and just a hint of garlic. Everyone grows something, even in flowerpots along the street, in mini urban gardens. If you haven't harvested your own seeds, they're easy to buy in the markets like Lijiang's Zhonghi – packets and packets of them!

The variety in the markets is extraordinary, and there's a real respect for the whole plant: carrots come complete with fronds, and green beans complete with their lovely orange flowers. A typical soupy pumpkin village dish would include pumpkin leaves and pumpkin flowers. Barbecued vegetables – potato, sweet potato, bell peppers and heads of corn – are grilled on the street and eaten as snacks.

Fried Crispy Lotus Root with Garlic

Because the root is finely sliced, and the dish is dry (no water is added), be very careful with the cooking time and temperature.

INGREDIENTS

1 medium lotus root, peeled and very thinly sliced
2 tsp minced garlic
2 tsp chilli flakes
1 tsp salt
2 tsp oil, for frying

METHOD

1. Mix together garlic and chilli flakes
2. Heat the oil in a pan and fry lotus root wheels until the underside is browned and each piece is tender and translucent. Start with a medium heat and then bring the temperature down to low. Cover. The cooking time is 3-4 minutes
3. Turn the pieces, and stir in garlic, chilli and salt, coating each wheel. Serve hot

Cabbage & Pumpkin with Tomato Salsa

Freshness and flavour are the keys to southern Yunnan food. Crispy, just-harvested cabbage is served with a tingling delicious tomato salad. You can also use seasonal baby spinach and cucumbers, julienned.

INGREDIENTS

½ round white cabbage, cut into chunks and cleaned

200 g / 7 oz pumpkin cubes

2 tsp fine chilli flakes

225 g / 8 oz tomato salsa (see page 24)

1 tsp oil, for frying

METHOD

1. Heat the oil in a pan and fry pumpkin until golden brown, with a sprinkling of chilli flakes
2. Serve hot with the chilled cabbage and a dish of tomato salsa

Naxi Stir-Fried Potatoes with Pickled Vegetables

INGREDIENTS

1 medium potato, peeled, finely sliced and cut into 2.5 cm / 1 in "square" pieces

1 clove garlic, finely sliced

2 tbsp pickled vegetables, chopped

2 tbsp oil, for frying

Salt, to taste

METHOD

1. In a wok, heat the oil and stir-fry the garlic. Add potatoes and cook for about 10 minutes, stirring regularly
2. Add pickled vegetables. Check for salt, and serve

Chinese Cabbage with Dried Chillies

Chinese cabbage is the tall, pale green cabbage with thick white stalks and frilly leaves. This is a simple, traditional village dish which brings out the full flavour of each of the ingredients: sweet seasonal cabbage, peppery ginger, and the kick of dried chillies. For extra flavour – and sheen – drizzle 1 tsp of sesame oil over the plated cabbage.

INGREDIENTS

½ Chinese cabbage, cut in two lengthwise
3 dried chillies
Large knob ginger, sliced
100 ml / 3½ fl oz water
Oil, for frying

METHOD

1. Wash the cabbage leaves and separate the stalks from the leaves
2. Cut the stalks into two lengthwise, and then into finger-sized strips. Chop the leafy part to the same size. Keep separate
3. Heat the oil in a pan and add chillies and ginger. Stir well. Add cabbage stalks and stir-fry for 1 minute
4. Add the water, bring to the boil, cover, and simmer for 3 minutes
5. Stir in leaves, stir, cover and cook for 2 minutes

Fried Eggplant with Dried Chillies

This traditional Yunnan dish calls for Asian eggplants – the long, thin version which are usually about 30 cm (12 in) long. For this recipe, the eggplants are peeled, the idea being to craft a soft, dry dish.

INGREDIENTS

2 Asian eggplants, peeled and cut into ½ cm / 1/5 in wheels
Salt, for rubbing
2 dried chillies
2 cloves garlic, crushed
1 tbsp oil, for frying
100 ml / 3½ fl oz water

METHOD

1. Roll the eggplant pieces in salt, rinse in water, and drain well
2. Heat the oil in a pan and stir in chillies
3. Add eggplant pieces and stir-fry, then add the garlic and stir-fry for a further 2 minutes
4. Add the water, bring to the boil, cover, and simmer for about 4 minutes until the eggplant is tender. Ensure that the water does not entirely evaporate

Tofu with Chinese Cabbage

INGREDIENTS

½ Chinese cabbage
100 g / 3½ oz deep-fried tofu
100 g / 3½ oz soft tofu
Knob ginger, sliced
2 dried chillies
100 ml / 3½ fl oz water
Oil, for frying

METHOD

1. Cut the cabbage into six chunks, then cut again lengthwise. Keep stalks separate
2. Heat some oil in a pan and fry ginger, chillies and stalks. Stir-fry for 3 minutes, then add the water. Cover, and simmer for 10 minutes
3. Cut the deep-fried tofu block in half, and slice the soft one. Add the deep-fried one to the pan and cook for a further 10 minutes
4. Lay the soft tofu slices on the deep-fried tofu, cover, and poach for 2 or 3 minutes. Add more water if necessary. Serve immediately

Potato & Yam with Crunchy Green Peppers

This dish beautifully brings together the best flavours of potato, yam and long, slim green peppers. It is very simple to put together, and tastes best when the root vegetables are in season, and the peppers are spicy-sweet to the taste. This dish is neither wet nor dry, but the peppers should remain crunchy. It is traditional to use a large amount of oil, but it is fine to use a mixture of oil and water.

INGREDIENTS

2 medium potatoes, peeled
1 medium taro, peeled
4 green peppers
4 cloves garlic, crushed
4 red chillies, finely chopped
100 ml / 3½ fl oz oil, or 2 tbsp oil with 100 ml / 3½ fl oz water
2 tsp salt

METHOD

1. Cut the potato, taro and peppers into uniform, bite-sized pieces
2. Heat oil in a pan, add garlic and chillies with potato and taro, and cook for 4 minutes until soft
3. Add peppers and fry for a further 2 minutes, ensuring the peppers are still crisp and brightly coloured. Serve hot

"Grandma's Potatoes"

This legendary dish looks so simple based on the list of ingredients, and in fact it is. The trick is to "crush" the potatoes not with an ordinary potato masher or even a knife, but to squeeze the potato into rough chunks through your fingers. It can be eaten at breakfast with bacon and eggs, or as a side dish with any meal.

INGREDIENTS

2 medium potatoes, peeled
1 tbsp salt
4 spring onions, finely chopped (green and white parts)
3 tbsp oil, for frying

METHOD

1. Quarter the potatoes, and boil in salted water for about 20 minutes until cooked but firm. Drain and dry. Squeeze into chunks by hand
2. Heat the oil in a wok and add spring onion. Stir for 1-2 minutes, then add potato and stir until well coated. Serve

The Bai Chef

In a small Dali market away from the tourist centre, holding a couple of the little baskets traditionally used to store tea at home, Chef Zhang Li Fen is buying ingredients for a cooking class. With merely a glance, she dismisses the wild-picked mushrooms at the stall on the steps outside the market, saying she will look around.

She buys a grey-skinned chicken ready for demonstrating a classic Bai dish, Hot and Sour Chicken Soup (one of her favourites), and then spies a stall selling all kinds of very local vegetables. Here, the foraged mushrooms come up to standard and she carefully selects some "Seeing the Hand, It Becomes Green" mushrooms, saying that the best are those with the thinner caps relative to stalk thickness. They are so-called because when a finger touches the cap, a green finger mark appears!

Unsure where to buy *rushan* – the locally made rolls of creamy-yellow cow's milk cheese which is traditionally sliced and fried, then sprinkled with sugar – she wanders over to the stall manned by her sister-in-law, and seeks directions. Meanwhile she picks up a quince (known locally as something like sour papaya), some local green peppers (they are half-hot), and a little packet of preserved green chillies.

Li Fen comes from a family of chefs. As a child she had little interest in cooking, but when her brother and his wife opened a cooking school, and she witnessed how glorious and beautiful even everyday *jiaozi* dumplings could be, she was hooked.

Originally from Luxi County – which she thinks produces Yunnan ham of better quality than the feted Xianwei (in Luxi it is lightly smoked over the domestic stove, after being hung) – she moved to Kunming to study Yunnan cooking at the New Oriental Cooking School. Today, she cooks for 100 people every morning at the City Government Offices in Dali, and for 10 people every night – her extended Bai family. While Bai families in the village tend to live in separate houses, in the city they all live together.

In fact, Li Fen is not Bai but Han, and moved to Dali with her Bai husband who works in an architectural practice. She has totally embraced Bai culture, can speak the dialect for everyday conversation, and loves the sour-spicy nature of the cuisine. Even people from her hometown, she says, love its fragrance and its ability to stimulate the appetite. Her story is not an unusual one – of a Han marrying into one of the ethnic minorities and becoming totally integrated.

Watching her chop, listening to her talk about cooking, and observing her total ease with what's in the pot, or the wok, her natural ability and quiet passion are clear. Even in this casual environment, every ingredient is elegantly chopped, and the set of ingredients for each dish precisely laid out on separate plates. The chicken, after being chopped into bite-sized pieces (skin on, bone in), is soaked in water to remove any blood traces, but she says how, if the weather is cold, the soaking water should be at least 30 degrees. This chicken will be cooked until the "taste of the bone" comes out.

Yunnan ham, she comments, can be used in just about any dish, in small quantities, to add a little flavour, as can a small scattering of Sichuan peppercorns. She explains that the reason for using so much garlic when cooking mushrooms (at least one sliced clove of garlic per person) is that if it turns black, you'll know that the mushrooms are poisonous. As it happens, stories of being poisoned by mushrooms are not exactly rare. □

Lunch at Fuxian Lake

One-and-a-half hours out of Kunming: Pick your own strawberries! In a plot just across from the ornate entrance to a Muslim village, strawberries ripen beautifully for three months of the year. Price: 20 yuan for half a kilo. But that's at least twice as much as in the Cheng Jiang market. Forget that! Onwards, then, to Fuxian Lake – first picking up a couple of bottles of Yunnan Red's "Rose Honey" wine at a corner store where the owner's puppy has a penchant for licking feet – to find somewhere for lunch.

The driver descends on a road straddled by steep, forested slopes in myriad shades of muted browns and greens, where swirls of smoke wind between village houses. These slopes are punctuated by only a few hard-to-reach terraces where corn is grown.

Fuxian is the third largest lake in Yunnan after Dianchi and Erhai, and the third deepest in China. It covers 212 square kilometres and measures 31.5 km by 11.5 km at its longest and widest points. Being near it is like being by the ocean, with an impactful water-meets-sky horizon. While it is home to a number of native fish species, Fuxian is most famous for the Kanglang, a fish which locals hold in total awe. It takes up to eight years for this creature to reach its

optimal 12 inches in length. The fish was prolific in the 1990s but, because of overfishing, is now rare – and very expensive. Government policies determine that fishing in this lake is allowed for just one month of the year, that being December.

So arriving lakeside on an intensely hot April day, the waves gently lapping in a welcome breeze, there are no fishing boats, just a few paddle-your-own craft for tourist excursions. "Would you like fish from the lake, or from the dam?" is the first question asked on entering the spacious restaurant. It is quiet here today in mid-week. Business is brisk at the weekend when what seems like half the residents of Kunming arrive. They're apparently not much liked, being regarded as noisy and rude, but they sure like to spend money. The owner's German Shepherd is having his tummy tickled, and the mynah bird is singing to an enthralled child who raises his arms towards the music. There's a table of four men – fishermen, judging by their weathered skins and sinewy limbs – drinking tea and playing cards.

Lake fish would be fantastic, we decide. A black carp is selected – but the price is 120 yuan per half a kilo, it is whispered. No problem.

The lively creature is rushed, protesting, from fish tank to chopping board, where it is clubbed and de-scaled, the flesh then scored to the skin. Into a copper pot filled with water it goes, where the flesh will simmer for just a few minutes.

Now, the owner's attention turns to another dish. A handful of whitebait is tossed by chopsticks with two eggs and at least a cup of potato starch in a small metal bowl. A little water is added. A wok is fired up, heating a substantial amount of oil, and then in goes the whitebait mix, slowly, in a fascinating movement reminiscent of spinning candy cane. It's drained and turned onto a plate: an omelette with "edges".

Meanwhile, Grandad is in charge of the potato rice, a traditional village dish now gentrified. Half-cooked rice goes into another copper pot with deep-fried potatoes, in some of their oil, and specks of Yunnan ham. It is covered. He wanders over to the fish and adds a teaspoon of salt, a little ginger, and some sprigs of highly aromatic coriander. That's it. A simple but utterly delicious dish – made possible only by using the best ingredients.

Edible young ferns, from the adjacent mountain sides, are chopped into two-inch lengths and quickly stir-fried with shredded spring onion. They present an almost nutty flavour and retain just a hint of crunch.

And then there's the *zha*, a special name for a pork and radish (or eggplant) dish unique to Yunnan. It

tastes intensely sour, the preserved radish having completely infused the pork skin. Eggplant absorbs the fat from the pork, creating a similarly delicious dish. Local women from the village, it is said, must know how to make this dish, otherwise no one will marry them.

Back at the shore, four or five Kanglang have come in, to a spot where spring water meets lake water, to lay their eggs. They have not gone unnoticed. □

MEAT AND POULTRY

In the mountainous, high-altitude northern parts of Yunnan, yak (not quite gamey but stronger than beef) and goat are the most commonly eaten meats. But in the south, pork is preferred. The pork section of the market is the most active and atmospheric, the competition intense among stallholders.

However, there's invariably a long line of cages of all kinds of ducks and chickens, often the base of highly nutritious, healthy stocks. Some farms rear pheasants and pigeons for specialist restaurants and private clients.

Aromatic Lemon Honey Chicken

This recipe calls for chicken "Marylands" – the thigh and drumsticks. It is amazingly aromatic, and incorporates so many classic Yunnan flavours all in one go.

INGREDIENTS

2 chicken "Marylands", washed and patted dry
2 stalks lemongrass, sliced into 3 cm/1 in pieces
4 dried chillies • 2 star anise
1 tbsp peppercorns
4 black cardamom
4 cloves garlic
2 slices ginger
125 ml / 4½ fl oz Chinese cooking wine
175 ml / 6 fl oz dark soy sauce
1 tbsp tamarind pulp
Water, as required • 1 tbsp honey
2 slices fresh lemon • 1 tsp oil, for frying

METHOD

1. In a dry pan, roast lemongrass, chillies, star anise, peppercorns and cardamoms until aromatic
2. Add oil to the pan, and blister ginger and garlic
3. Add wine and simmer for 5 minutes
4. Add soy sauce, tamarind and chicken, with just enough water to cover the chicken. Simmer for 5 minutes, then turn chicken, add honey and lemon, bring to the boil and simmer for a further 7 minutes. Turn the heat off and allow the chicken to sit for 2 hours
5. Reheat before serving

Braised Pork Belly with Bitter Melon

This dish is more about the bitter melon than the pork, as it fully absorbs the meat flavours. The most traditional vegetable to use is bitter melon, though villagers might use taro. A modern version would feature potato. Both alternatives are shown here, and the cooking time is the same.

INGREDIENTS

500 g / 1 lb 2 oz pork belly, cut into two
1 tbsp soy sauce
2 dried chillies
225 ml / 8 fl oz water
4 bitter melons, peeled and cored and chunkily cut into about 4 pieces
Oil, for browning and frying

METHOD

1. Heat some oil in a pan and, skin down, brown one piece of the pork. Brown on each side, about 5 minutes per side. Repeat for the second piece of pork. Set aside
2. Heat a little more oil in another pan, and add the pork. Stir in soy sauce, chillies, water and bitter melon. Bring to the boil, cover, and simmer for 45 minutes until both the meat and the vegetables are tender

If using potatoes:

Peel 4 medium potatoes (about 500 g / 1 lb 2 oz), halve them, and add 1 tsp salt

If using taro:

Peel 4 small taro (about 500 g / 1 lb 2 oz) and cut into chunky pieces about 6 cm x 3 cm x 3 cm / 2 in x 1 in x 1 in deep. Add 1 tsp salt

Pork & Water Chestnut Patties

It's autumn and water chestnuts are in season, piled high on the streets of Kunming. Visiting Hong Kong, Linda finds them in the market, too, and creates this dish, fully reflecting the "flavours of Yunnan" but drawing on her Cantonese heritage. What could be more Yunnan than chestnuts and pig? Traditionally, Yunnan people use potato and cornflour, but plain flour can be used here. These are excellent paired with any of the core Yunnan dips (page 24). The same mixture, more or less, can be used to stuff preserved mustard greens, and is shown below.

INGREDIENTS

200 g / 7 oz lean pork meat • 4 water chestnuts, finely diced
3 tbsp finely chopped red onion • 1 tbsp finely chopped shallots
1 tbsp finely chopped spring onion (green part) • 1 tsp finely chopped garlic
2 tsp light soy sauce • 2 tsp ground dried chilli
1 egg, beaten • 1 tbsp flour
Flour, for dusting • Oil, for frying

METHOD

1. Combine all the ingredients, except egg and flour, and work the mixture until it is thick and pliable. Add the egg, mix well, then stir in the flour
2. Take 1 tbsp of the paste, form into a ball, roll in flour, then flatten into a patty shape
3. Heat about 1 tbsp of oil in a pan over a high heat, add patties, turn down the heat and fry for about 3 minutes each side

For pork-stuffed mustard leaves:

Make the mixture as above, but instead of water chestnuts, use canned bamboo shoots, chopped finely. Take a cabbage leaf, place 2 tsp of the mixture at the centre, fold in sides, then roll tightly. Steam for 20 minutes

Eight Treasures Chicken

This autumn dish (symbolised by the chestnuts) is a favourite for celebrating good health and fortune. Optional ingredients include smoked dried oysters, and on very special occasions would feature duck instead of chicken.

INGREDIENTS

1 small chicken (about 1.5 kg / 3 lb 5 oz) • 7.5 cm / 3 in piece ginger, crushed
3 medium shallots, halved • 1 tsp light soy sauce
125 ml / 4½ fl oz Chinese cooking wine
4 black cardamom • 6 dried chillies • 8 shiitake mushrooms, soaked overnight
Handful dried bak choi, soaked for 2 hours • Handful wood fungus, soaked for 2 hours
1 tsp salt • 1 tsp dark soy sauce • 2 tbsp Chinese vinegar
10 chestnuts, boiled for 3 minutes, then peeled and halved • 225 ml / 8 fl oz water
3 small taro roots, peeled and cut into bite-sized pieces
1 bamboo shoot (canned), cut into bite sized pieces • 3 tsp freshly ground black pepper
125 g / 4½ oz goji berries, soaked for 2 hours • 125 g / 4½ oz dried longans, soaked for 2 hours
4 red dates, soaked for 2 hours • 2 tsp oil, for frying

METHOD

1. Clean the chicken, and cut it into bite-sized pieces. Rinse with hot water, dry, and then place in a large bowl with ginger, shallots, light soy sauce and wine and rest for 30 minutes
2. Heat oil in a large saucepan and stir-fry cardamoms, chilli, mushrooms and bak choi with salt. Add the dark soy sauce
3. Add chicken and vinegar and stir-fry for 5 minutes
4. Add chestnuts and the water. Add taro, bak choi and bamboo shoots with the pepper, and braise for 10 minutes
5. Add dried fruits and braise for a further 10 minutes. Serve hot

Steamed Pork Balls on Banana Leaf

The traditional way to prepare the meat mixture is on a chopping board, slowly working the ingredients in the pork by constantly folding the outside edges to the centre with a cleaver. The ingredients can also be mixed together in a bowl by hand. These balls are also delicious steamed on a thin slice of Yunnan ham, and make for impressive party food.

INGREDIENTS

1 banana leaf
500 g / 1 lb 2 oz minced pork
100 g / 3½ oz preserved vegetables, finely chopped
100 g / 3½ oz Chinese cabbage leaves, finely chopped
4 small green chillies, finely chopped
200 g / 7 oz soft tofu, finely chopped
1 tbsp finely chopped coriander leaves
1 tbsp soy sauce
2 shallots, finely chopped
5 cm / 2 in piece ginger, finely chopped
1 tsp salt
1 tsp freshly ground black pepper

METHOD

1. Wash the banana leaf and cut into 4 cm / 1½ inch squares. Set aside
2. Carefully mix together all the other ingredients
3. In the palm of your hand, form a tablespoonful of mixture into a ball
4. Place the balls on the banana leaf squares and steam for 20 minutes

Pork Loin with Mustard Greens & Preserved Vegetables

This is a modern Yunnan recipe. Any seasonal greens can be used, but only incorporate preserved vegetables if you are preparing this dish with mustard greens (because the preserved vegetable is also mustard greens). Broccoli, for example, doesn't work with these preserved vegetables.

INGREDIENTS

200 g / 7 oz pork loin, thinly sliced
1 bunch mustard greens (about 3 pieces)
Knob ginger, sliced
2 tsp light soy sauce
1 tsp salt
Pinch pepper
125 ml / 4½ fl oz water
1 tbsp preserved vegetables
Oil, for frying

METHOD

1. Wash the greens and cut both stalks and leaves into bite-sized pieces, keeping the two separate
2. Heat a little oil in a pan and stir-fry pork until just cooked. Set aside
3. Put a little more oil in the pan, and add ginger, soy sauce, salt and pepper and the stems. Stir-fry for 2 minutes
4. Stir in the leafy part, with the water. Cover, and cook for 1 minute
5. Stir in the preserved vegetables, then the pork

Roast Pork Rib with Chilli Bean Paste

This modern pork rib dish was inspired by barbecued pork chops cooked on the street.

INGREDIENTS

1.5 kg / 3 lb 5 oz pork belly with ribs attached

1 tbsp black bean paste

1 tbsp chilli bean paste

4 cloves garlic, smashed

1 tbsp lemon juice

1 tbsp oil

1 tsp garam masala

1 tsp chilli flakes

METHOD

1. Clean the meat, removing the skin. Cut into long pieces following the rib bone
2. Mix together the pastes with garlic, lemon juice and oil. Spread this marinade all over the ribs and let sit for 2 hours
3. Pre-heat the oven to 200°C / 400°F. Roast the pork for 15-20 minutes
4. Turn the pork, and reduce to 160°C / 320°F, and roast for 1 hour until the cut is succulent inside and crispy on the outside. Baste now and again
5. Serve sprinkled with garam masala and chilli flakes

Pork Stewed with Autumn Melon

The rather bland melon absorbs the flavour of the pork. All kinds of melons – winter, autumn or otherwise – can be used. The proportion of "cooling" melon to "heating" ginger is important. This dish has a stew-like consistency.

INGREDIENTS

100 g / 3½ oz lean pork, finely sliced against the grain into thin strips
125 g / 4½ oz autumn melon, finely sliced into pieces about 3 cm x 2 cm / 1 in x ¾ in
2 cm / ¾ in knob ginger, finely chopped
2 tbsp water
Salt, to taste
1 tbsp oil, for frying

METHOD

1. Heat the oil, stir-fry ginger and then place melon on one side of the wok, and the pork on the other
2. Remove pork as soon as it is translucent. Fry melon, then add water and a pinch of salt. Cook until soft
3. Return pork to the pan, adding water as necessary

Stuffed Banana Leaf

If you are unable to get banana leaves with which to create this Dai dish, use Chinese cabbage leaves. Wash, cut off the thick stems (use them for another dish), and blanch in salted water. Pat dry. Place about 2 tsps of filling towards the bottom of the leaf. Fold over the sides, then tightly roll. Obviously the whole thing can be eaten if using cabbage, rather than banana, leaf.

INGREDIENTS

200 g / 7 oz minced lean pork
100 g / 3½ oz tofu, finely chopped
100 g / 3½ oz red onion, finely chopped
50 g / 1¾ oz preserved vegetables, finely chopped
100 g / 3½ oz cabbage, finely chopped
2-3 tbsp finely chopped coriander leaves and stalks
1 spring onion, finely chopped
3 green chillies, finely chopped
1 tsp salt • 1 tsp freshly ground black pepper
Bunch of banana leaves • Tooth picks for sealing

METHOD

1. Lay out the pork on a board, and slowly work in all the other ingredients, folding the mixture with a chopper until everything is perfectly combined
2. Wash and clean banana leaves and cut into A4-size pieces
3. Fill leaves with 1 tbsp of the filling, fold the leaf around the filling and seal with toothpicks
4. Steam for 20 minutes

Roasted Bell Peppers stuffed with Pork & Tofu

INGREDIENTS

4 bell peppers

200 g / 7 oz minced pork

1 tbsp preserved vegetables

100 g / 3½ oz tofu, roughly chopped

1 tsp Sichuan peppercorns, finely crushed

½ tsp salt

METHOD

1. Remove the heads of the bell peppers and set aside. Remove seeds and fibrous strips from the inside. Pat dry and set aside
2. Lay the pork on a chopping board, top with preserved vegetables, and "chop" the two together by folding in the meat from the outside
3. Add peppercorns and salt and mix well
4. Put this mixture into a bowl, and finely cut in the tofu. "Beat" the mixture with chopsticks for about 2 minutes until it is smooth. If it remains hard, add a splash of cold water
5. Stuff the peppers with this mixture, and put the heads back on
6. Pre-heat the oven to 200°C / 400°F, place peppers on a tray and roast for 10 minutes. Turn the heat down to 170°C / 340°F and roast for a further 35 minutes or until the meat is well cooked

Sliced Pork with Garlic Chives

Garlic chives have a very strong flavour, and one which is not universally popular. The best have a white part, just as spring onions do. This dish calls for pork, but can also be made with chicken. The incorporation of bean sprouts is more Cantonese than Yunnanese.

INGREDIENTS

300 g / 10½ oz pork loin (or 1 chicken breast), thinly sliced

2 tsp light soy sauce

Bunch flowering garlic chives (about 200 g / 7 oz), chopped into 5 cm / 2 in lengths (keep white and green parts separately)

6 spring onions, cut into 5 cm / 2 in lengths (keep white and green parts separately)

2 dried chillies, cut into 2 or 3 pieces diagonally

100 g / 3½ oz bean sprouts (optional)

Salt, to taste

Oil, for frying

METHOD

1. Marinate the pork (or chicken) in the soy sauce for 1 hour
2. Heat a little oil in a pan and stir-fry the meat until just cooked. Set aside
3. Add a little more oil and stir-fry the white part of the chives and spring onions with the chillies until the vegetables are transparent
4. Add green part of the chives and stir-fry for 1 minute, add the green part of the spring onions with bean sprouts and salt and stir-fry for ½ minute. Return the meat to the pan and stir-fry until combined

Stir-Fried Pork with Jicama & Asparagus Stalks

For this dish, use the tough ends of the asparagus stalks, reserving the tender tips for another dish.

INGREDIENTS

100 g / 3½ oz lean pork, finely sliced against the grain into thin strips
2 long thin green peppers (about 50 g), tips set aside, the remainder halved then julienned
100 g / 3½ oz jicama, peeled and julienned into 6 cm long pieces
4 thick asparagus stalks (tough part, not the tips), peeled and cut into pieces the same size as the jicama
2 chillies, halved lengthwise
1 clove garlic, finely sliced
25 g / 1 oz lalang grass rhizome, scraped and chopped into 2 cm / ¾ in lengths
Pinch Sichuan peppercorns
Salt and pepper, to taste
1 tbsp oil, for frying

METHOD

1. Heat oil in a wok, fry chillies, garlic, and the pepper tips
2. Move to one side of the wok and cook pork with a pinch of salt, stirring and pressing the meat down until translucent. Remove
3. Add jicama and peppers with a pinch of salt. Cook for 2 minutes, adding more oil as necessary
4. Add asparagus and cook for 1 minute
5. Replace pork, stir in lalang grass rhizome and peppercorns

Twice-Cooked Pork Belly with Kumquats

This dish works best with top quality organic pork. Browning locks in the juices and flavour of the pork. Prepare the dish at least 4 hours in advance – or even the night before.

INGREDIENTS

1 kg / 2 lb 4 oz pork belly, cleaned (any whiskers removed)
Salt, for sprinkling
3 cloves garlic, crushed • 2 slices ginger
4 shallots, crushed • 4 dried chillies
2 tsp Sichuan peppercorns, crushed
6 fresh kumquats • 2 tbsp soya bean paste
110 ml / 4 fl oz Chinese cooking wine • 1 tbsp honey
1 tsp black pepper • Salt, to sprinkle • Oil, for frying

METHOD

1. Heat some oil in a pan and fry the pork, skin down, pressing down in order for the fat to render. This can take up to 15 minutes. Repeat to brown the four sides, which takes about 20 minutes in total. Finally, gently brown the bottom side
2. Add garlic, ginger, shallots and chillies with a sprinkling of salt to the pan. Cover and allow to sit for 1 hour, or overnight
3. Over a medium heat, add peppercorns, kumquats, soya bean paste, half the wine and honey to the pan. Bring to the boil. Place meat skin down and simmer for 30 minutes. Add more wine to keep the sauce about halfway up the meat
4. Turn the meat and simmer for a further 30 minutes
5. Remove and carve the meat. Remove the kumquats and mash
6. Drain the sauce and, in a small pan, reduce it to a fine syrup. Add a little to the mashed kumquats and use the remainder to drizzle over the meat

"Toasted" Duck

People readily drive 15 minutes outside Yiliang city on a weekday to a restaurant where they might risk no parking space and, worse, no table at all. Diehards sit on the humble wall outside and eat their "toasted" duck there. In Chinese the dish literally translates as "Yiliang Toasted Duck" and it is a speciality of this city, some 45 minutes' drive from Kunming, and the closest city to the dramatic tourist attraction of the Stone Forest where Ashima is the most visited "stone".

This restaurant, named in direct translation "12 Animals – Goat" (the little town is known as North Goat Street), prepares something in the order of 1,000 ducks a day, and that's just on weekdays. The quality of the end product starts, of course, with the calibre of the duck itself. Here, they are reared in the rice paddies for four or five months, benefiting from the various insects and so on which live there. They're brightly coloured ducks – unlike the white Peking ducks – and about half the size.

After culling, the duck is first thoroughly washed and then hung out to dry. Each one is then massaged in a honey wash by skilled hands for about a minute, starting with a neck-stretching before every spot of the body is covered; and they are then left to marinate and dry in the gentle breeze. Meanwhile, giant clay ovens with front-loading doors and huge lids are being prepared. In one corner there's a pile of ropes which are burning material for the ovens: thickly twisted dried pine needles. When the fire has gone out, reduced to perfumed embers, it is time to lower in the ducks on hooks, eight at a time, each with a little dish below it to catch the grease. The chef, with burn marks all up his arms and a cigarette flopping from his mouth, roasts them for about 45 minutes, until the skins are brown and crispy.

Cleavered into about 12 pieces, the duck's accompaniments are a sweetish bean sauce and hearty lengths of raw spring onion, the white part only. The duck skin is dark in colour (because of the honey) and ultimately crispy. Unlike Peking duck, there's not a trace of fat and the meat is dense and rich, but tender and moist. The meat is simply eaten in hunks, with little sides of pickled cabbage, baby turnips and cucumber.

Driving back into town, there are plenty of similar-looking ovens wafting fragrant smoke onto the street, and rows of uniform ducks hang out on long metal bars. But the duck is not the right one, the honey is not the right one, the oven is not at the right heat, and the cooking time is imprecise. That's why people drive 15 minutes for lunch when they could walk three. □

Shangri-La

Broadcasted sounds of the danceable rhythms of traditional Tibetan music, with a certain 21st-century riff, waft through narrow cobbled streets (hazardously slippery when the clouds open) lined with myriad "westernised" bars and souvenir shops, some of the latter quite tasteful, offering yak-leather bags and ear-hugging woollen hats. There are one or two places selling all the kit one might need for a freezing cold trek to the nearby Tiger Leaping Gorge, and there's a knife shop, too.

This is the "Old City" of Shangri-La (pronounced Shanga-lee-la), a place that doesn't actually exist – or does it? This city used to be known as Zhongdian ("City of Sun and Moon"), and has traditionally been a place which Tibetans have considered a kind of paradise. It is not the most beautiful part of Yunnan, though the Shi Ka Snow Mountain has 13 peaks, but these don't dramatically frame the city like those of Jade Dragon Snow Mountain outside Lijiang. However, today's name of Shangri-La, assumed in 2003 as a marketing ploy, means "Sun and Moon in the Heart". This lovely phrase might indeed suggest more of an existential space of spiritual enlightenment than a city with beautiful vistas. And the "Old City" was in fact only constructed in 2005. Dali has one, Lijiang has one – "So why not us?" is how the thinking presumably went.

The month is July and there's a distinct chill in the heavy evening air, but the squally rains have dissipated and a milling crowd awaits music-led action in the Old City's central square (known as Square Street).

Here, earlier in the day, women have set up their food stalls, sending strands of smoke over low roofs from their diddy little charcoal-fired barbecues, and slipping all manner of produce onto sticks: yak meat, pork, mutton, tofu, mushrooms and so on. In spite of the relatively large number of tourists around, almost all the takers here are local. Local people are populating their own central square, bringing a lovely sense of community. The Old City may look to have been created for tourists, yet there's a cultural integrity about it. And then, as light falls, the vendors pack up. For now it is time to dance.

The square's patterned paving forms a series of concentric rings to facilitate Tibetan dancing. On the inner circle, there are a few much older women in traditional dress, moving clockwise in time with the music, their turning bodies a picture of elegance. The next layer has mostly men, of varying ages and sizes. And then comes a most delightful part. On the outer rings, people of many different nationalities, including children, sway gently in and out of the action and

attempt to copy the broad foot and arm movements of the Tibetans on the inner circles. A couple of tall blondes don't follow the moves exactly, but look quite lovely with their long hair flowing. There's again a sense of strong community, of Tibetans sharing their traditional dances without artifice (Tibetans love to sing, and to dance) with anyone who cares to join in, or simply observe this celebration from the square's edges. It is a moving experience.

Life is lived more in the raw at the downtown Nong Mau Market on the famous Low March Road, though the market is spacious, calm and regularly washed down. One weathered butcher has on offer a huge slab of meat, almost cone-shaped, which turns out to be a yak neck, weighing in at an amazing 300 kilos. The poultry corner is a live performance of neck slitting, after which chickens are thrown into a machine which automatically removes their feathers, though ducks are hand-plucked. They are carefully eviscerated. In the pork section, slabs of meat are set to with a blowtorch, to remove any thick hairs, by a butcher in a black plastic apron with a cigarette stuck to his lower lip. Things are more peaceful in the beef area: three vendors are even playing a board game amid the various cuts.

Traditionally dressed grandmothers have breakfast with their grandchildren. One little girl, not even a year old, has pierced ears and her wrists are laden with silver jewellery. For many here, breakfast is a simple bowl of congee (to which salt and/or sugar is added) and a round of *baba* bread.

A couple of guys come in among the lush vegetable stalls with woven plastic baskets on their backs, clearly buying produce for restaurants. They leave with heavy, overflowing loads. In a back corner, a lady sells traditional baskets for vegetables, and Tibetan pottery. Close to the entrance, a young man sells copper water-lading pots and, strung on ropes, traditional yak bells – originals (more expensive) and copies. Gently brush a row of them and they stretch to a whole musical scale. Just like the music in the square.

Terry, who is Naxi, loves Shangri-La. The food, the music, the dancing and especially the Matsutake mushrooms now in season. Better than any mushroom dishes she's had at home around Lijiang, she declares. Would she like to have a Tibetan boyfriend? Oh yes, but the problem is, she gets the idea that Tibetans don't shower very often and she holds personal cleanliness rather highly in a partner – even above money and work ethic. So for now at least she simply observes the culture, and picks up another Tibetan CD to listen to in the car on her way home. □

YUNNAN HAM

Yunnan ham is the province's most famous product, and is used in so many ways. It lends a delicious flavour to simple bean, rice or potato dishes, and the fat part is used to cook vegetables. The lean and fat parts are sometimes combined in a single dish. The ham can also be eaten raw.

A number of artisan farmers are now producing meat which is reaching the sophistication of Parma ham (Italy), Iberico ham (Spain) or Pata Negre (Portugal), and its production is as much a family affair as a commercial one. When the air's dry and there's a breeze, hocks hang. The very best are those left to age in special basements with a very specific climatic condition.

The highest-quality meat is traditionally said to come from the area of Xuanwei – Xuanwei ham is almost synonymous with Yunnan ham – and the best producer is often cited as the family of Deng Xiaoping's wife. But gourmets today have discovered the ham produced from a little black pig which roams freely on the banks of the Nujiang River, way up in the northwest of the province. This pig drinks from natural springs and runs free, grazing on an all-organic diet.

Steamed Yunnan Ham with Taro and Tofu

These are gorgeous-looking steamed snacks, with taro at the bottom, tofu on top, and ham in the middle. The flavours emanate from the ham. This makes about 12 pieces. Serve with any of the dips shown on page 24.

INGREDIENTS

1 taro, peeled and sliced into 2.5 cm / 1 in wheels, about ½ cm / ¼ in thick
50 g / 1¾ oz Yunnan ham, lean part with a little fat, finely sliced to about the same size
20 g / 1 oz tofu, cut into about the same size with 1 cm / ½ in thickness
Slices of leek, for garnish
Bird's-eye chillies, for garnish

METHOD

1. Taking great care, assemble the snacks with taro, followed by ham, followed by tofu
2. Top each with a slice of leek and a bird's-eye chilli
3. Steam for 20 minutes

Yunnan Ham with Eggplant and Capsicum

This dish uses the very fat part of the ham. The proportions of red capsicum and green capsicum to eggplant should be about one third of each. In Yunnan, a typical cook would use 10 times the amount of oil shown here: this recipe is rather more conservative. The crisp capsicum is wonderfully fragrant, and the eggplant takes on the smokiness of the ham, with an overall fresh taste and peppery finish. The dish comes together best when the eggplant is of high quality.

INGREDIENTS

10 g / ½ oz Yunnan ham, fat part
½ red capsicum, cut into 2.5 cm / 1 in squares
½ green capsicum, cut into 2.5 cm / 1 in squares
75 g / 2¾ oz slim eggplant, cut into 1 cm / ½ in wheels
1 tsp finely chopped garlic
½ tsp salt
½ tsp pepper
½ tbsp oil, for frying

METHOD

1. Heat the oil and render the fat. On the other side of the pan, fry garlic (taking care not to burn it) and add the eggplant pieces followed by the capsicum. Stir everything together and cook for 2 minutes. Add salt and pepper
2. Turn the heat down and stir-fry for 2 minutes. Cover and cook for a further minute or so, ensuring that the capsicum remains crisp

Yunnan Ham stuffed Lotus Root

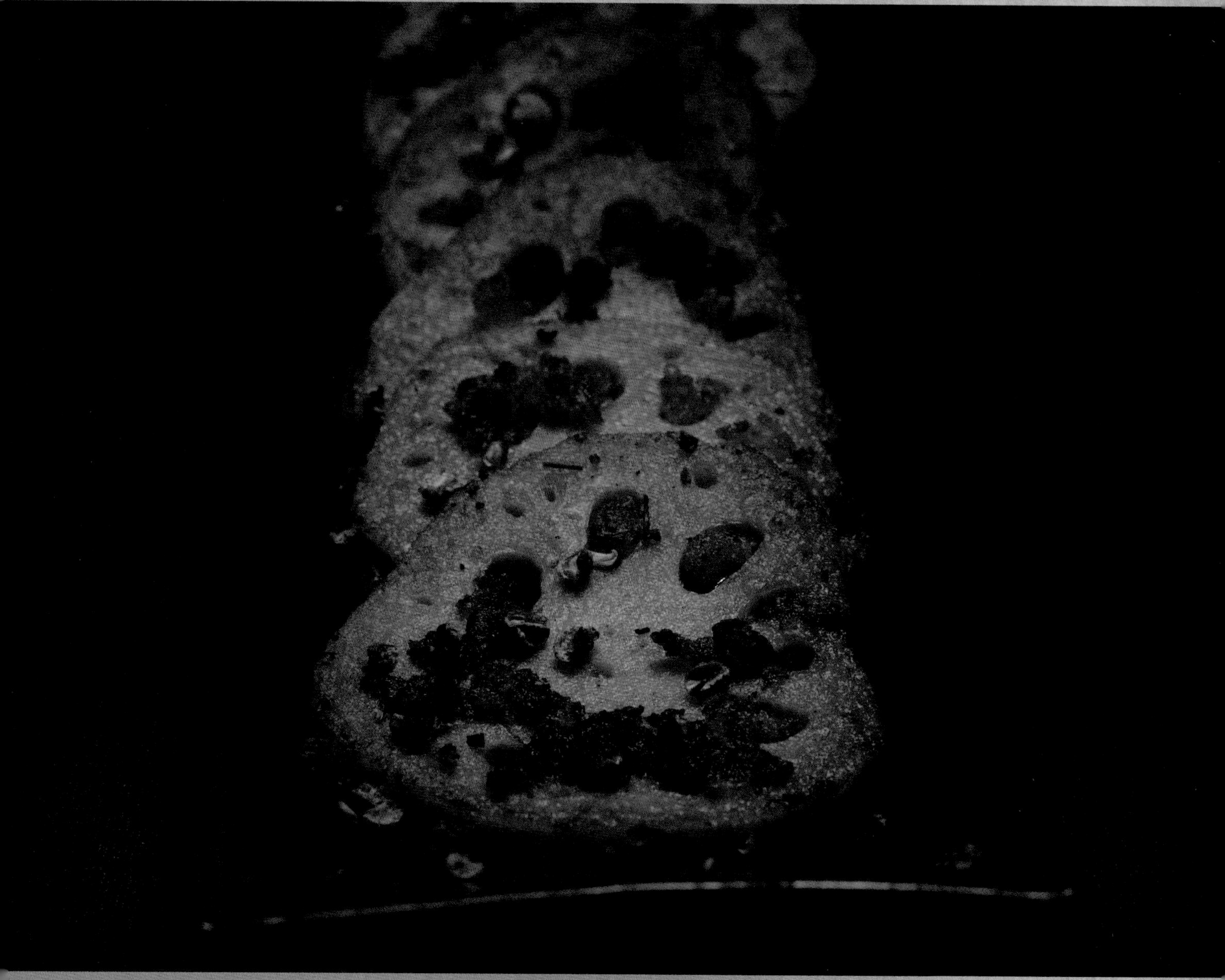

This dish sounds a bit fiddly, but is absolutely delicious and worth the effort, and universally appealing. The aromas when the cooking is complete are amazing: caramelised sugar ameliorating the pork smell. This recipe does not turn the wheels, but they can readily be fried on both sides, becoming almost bacon-like.

INGREDIENTS

1 lotus root (about 9 cm / 3 in diameter), cut into ½ cm / 1/5 inch thick wheels

50 g / 1¾ oz lean ham, finely chopped

25 g / 1 oz fat ham, finely chopped

1 tsp finely chopped garlic

1 tsp finely chopped shallot

Generous pinch salt

½ tsp pepper

1 tbsp oil, for frying

METHOD

1. Squash together all the ingredients (except the oil) to make the paste with which to stuff the lotus root
2. Stuff the mixture into the holes, and create a thin layer of the paste on the top
3. Heat the oil until just sizzling, and fry the slices (paste side up) for 1 minute. There may be a little burn because of the sugar content in the lotus root
4. Place a see-through lid on the pan and turn the heat down a little. The oil should be sizzling but not burning the wheels. The lotus will become translucent
5. After about 7 minutes remove the lid, and turn the heat up. Cook until the water has evaporated. The slices should be a little browned on the bottom

The Naxi Restaurant Owner

It all started when hungry tourists would discreetly eye what the family in *that* house was having for dinner. It is a lovely property in the heart of Shuhe Old City (effectively part of Lijiang), along a cobbled lane, not far from the bridge with the ancient and famously smooth and shiny stones running down its centre. Tourists would ask where they could get some of *that* food with *those* aromas and *those* colours. And so, in a city which is home to 300,000 Naxi people, the Naxi restaurant Tian Han Ge was born in 2002, well ahead of the slow Lijiang tourism push which was later to emerge.

It's a cool February evening. Hanging in the central courtyard from wooden beams, and even trees, are sides and legs and bellies of pork. The climatic atmosphere is so dry that pork can dry naturally and perfectly, as can many vegetables which can then be preserved. The restaurant has just three tables, though there are extra spots on the terrace by the waterways, and also in the courtyard, though the latter is shared with a number of cats and tends to be populated by locals hanging out and playing cards.

In the restaurant, empty beer bottles stack up. Diners physically fight over who is to get the bill (apparently this is a local sport). Cigarette smoke hangs in the air. A woman peers in as she buys a hand-made purse in the store across the street. A dog wanders in. Tourists pass by.

Over pig-blood and rice sausage dipped in powdered cinnamon (or, even better, chilli paste), possibly the best pan-fried lentil cake to be had, and a remarkable chicken soup that tastes like chicken *used* to taste, the conversation turns to how great the vegetable dishes are in Naxi culture. And is it true that Tian Han Ge is the best Naxi restaurant in Shuhe?

Bright-eyed owner Bai Yue An smiles. She doesn't use as much soy sauce as other people, she says. She's looking for "true" flavours. But she doesn't do "bland" either. She does "Naxi flavour".

Given that the restaurant business is notoriously hard to make money in, and she employs four staff, how does she run things? She talks of ethics. In her restaurant, she says, every client is charged the same price. Certainly the restaurant food here is quite complex when compared with village cooking. And the cooking goes further. The delicious steamed fish suggests some influence from Cantonese cuisine; and glutinous rice steamed in tubes of bamboo is right out of the Dai canon.

Before she opened the restaurant, she was a farmer with about six *mu* of land (that's almost a football pitch). She sold much of it to the government (who then sold it to Banyan Tree for their Shuhe resort) and she now has about two *mu*, which she rents out. She also owns a 10-room guesthouse, but she's too busy to run it. When the Banyan Tree property was being built, she let out the place to all the engineers. Each was charged 5,000 yuan per year. And now she has purchased a small apartment in Kunming, currently the residence of her second daughter.

Did she ever believe she would have such success? Never, she says. She adds that "other" people have money and now she does, too. Never in her wildest dreams would she have anticipated this kind of wealth. Does wealth equate to happiness? Of course, she says.

Do Naxi women wear the trousers? Naxi husbands are notoriously lazy. But there's a saying which suggests that Naxi women, though very hardworking, can't dream of their men being tired at night.

What of Bai Yue An's own husband? He washes the dishes in the restaurant, apparently, but after further investigation it turns out that he also goes to market to buy ingredients: the things which the family doesn't grow or nurture themselves. They are both 50 years old. She looks years older and rural. He looks years younger and urban. No wonder she doesn't want to tire him out. □

FISH AND SEAFOOD

Dai grilled fish scented with lemongrass and fresh herbs is one of the great fish dishes of Yunnan, alongside the Bai fish stew made with carp from Dali's commanding Erhai Lake. The fish from Yunnan's majestic lakes are generally highly prized. It is a land-locked province, and so it is unusual to find seafood and salt-water fish, but the small, often bony fish from the river show up in soups, or are coated in cornflour, then lightly fried. In general, fish does not figure highly in village cooking.

Shrimps with Garlic Chives

Use small, tasty shrimps for this dish, perhaps removing just the head and the legs but not the shell.

INGREDIENTS

500 g / 1 lb 2 oz shrimps, cleaned and deveined
1 bunch flowering garlic chives (about 200 g / 7 oz), cut into 3 cm / 1 in lengths
1 bunch yellow garlic chives (about 200 g / 7oz), cut into 3 cm / 1 in lengths
Salt, to taste
2 tbsp oil, for frying

METHOD

1. Heat the oil in a pan and, over a high heat, stir-fry shrimps until transparent
2. Add chives with some salt and stir to combine

Dai Grilled Fish with Lemongrass

This is a favourite, classic Dai dish. Traditionally it is prepared over burning coals, which lends an appealing smoky character to the fish as it browns and turns a little crunchy. It can also be served cold, with chilli chutney (see page 20) and tomato salsa (see page 24). The fish can also be pan-fried (choose a fish which fits snugly in your pan!), grilled in the oven, or baked in the oven.

INGREDIENTS

1 whole fish, scaled, gutted and cleaned
2 stalks lemongrass, halved lengthwise
For the marinade:
2 spring onions, finely chopped
2 sprigs of garlic chives, finely chopped
2 cloves garlic, finely chopped
2 sprigs of mint
2 sprigs of coriander
2 stalks lemongrass
1 knob ginger, finely chopped
1 tbsp chilli paste
Pinch salt
Salt, to sprinkle

METHOD

1. Cut the fish in half horizontally to fan it out
2. Mash together the marinade ingredients (this is traditionally done with bamboo pestle and mortar)
3. Place half in the cavity, and the other half on a plate. Lay the fish on it, cover, and rest in the fridge for 1 hour

(continued...)

4. Remove fish from the fridge, sprinkle with salt, lay the lemongrass pieces across it, and clamp it with a BBQ grill. Barbecue for about 3 minutes on each side until cooked

For grilling in the oven

After an hour in the fridge, place the stuffed fish under the grill and cook on each side for about 4 minutes

For oven-baking

Pre-heat the oven to 200°C / 400°F. Drizzle an oven-proof pan with olive oil, and place 3 lemon slices at the bottom, top with lemongrass. Lay the fish on the top of these. Cover the fish with foil or paper. Reduce the oven temperature to 170°C / 340°F and bake for 50 minutes. Serve hot

For pan-frying

Coat the fish with a little cornflour and fry in a hot pan for 2 minutes until browned. Reduce the fire and cook for a further 5 minutes. Bring the heat up again, turn the fish, and cook for 1 minute. Reduce the heat and cook for a further 5 minutes. Garnish with sprigs of mint and coriander and serve

Fish and Tofu Hot Pot

This is a deeply satisfying dish with a densely flavoured broth and lovely contrasts: sourness from the tomato and preserved vegetables, and a complex spiciness from the chilli, peppercorns and black pepper. Grass carp works well.

INGREDIENTS

200 g / 7 oz freshwater fish fillet
200 g / 7 oz tofu, sliced
2 thick slices ginger, crushed
3 spring onions, white part
2 tbsp preserved vegetables
½ green tomato, thickly sliced
1 large dried chilli, sliced diagonally into 3 pieces
2 tsp Sichuan peppercorns
1 tsp black pepper
Pinch salt

METHOD

1. Place fish in a clay pot with ginger, spring onion and preserved vegetables. Cover with water. Bring to the boil, cover, and simmer for 30 minutes
2. Add tomato, chilli, and peppers. Simmer for a further 10 minutes
3. Add tofu with salt, simmer for 2 minutes

Fish with Lotus Root & Tofu in Clay Pot

This is a traditional Dai dish where the main taste is the preserved vegetables. The fish poaches on the top, allowing for a dish which is both fresh and flavoursome.

INGREDIENTS

300 g / 10½ oz fish fillet, washed and patted dry

Small lotus root, peeled and cut into 6 thin wheels, then halved (about 200 g / 7 oz in weight)

100 g / 3½ oz tofu, cut into pieces the same size as the lotus root

1 knob ginger

1½ tbsp preserved vegetables

2 dried chillies

4 spring onions, white part cut into 3 cm / 1 in pieces; green part finely chopped

1 tsp salt

700 ml / 1½ pints water

2 tsp oil, for frying

METHOD

1. Heat 2 tsp of oil in a pan, add ginger, preserved vegetables, chillies and the white part of the spring onions, and stir well until sizzling and aromatic
2. Add salt and water and bring to the boil. Add lotus root, stir well, bring back to the boil, cover, lower heat, and simmer for 10 minutes
3. Add fish, bring back to the boil, cover, and simmer for 10 minutes
4. Add tofu, bring back to the boil, add green part of spring onion, cover, and simmer for a further minute

Sauteed Fish with Dragon Fruit in Blacksalty Seeds

This is a somewhat modernised Akha dish, but using blacksalty seeds – the dried seeds from a tree which grows in Xishuangbanna. If you cannot access blacksalty seeds, substitute with a mix of 1 tsp ground black cardamom and ½ tsp Sichuan peppercorns.

INGREDIENTS

500 g / 1 lb 2 oz fish fillet, de-boned and cut into bite-sized pieces
1 tsp blacksalty seeds
Large knob ginger, finely chopped
2 shallots, finely sliced
1 dragon fruit, peeled and cut into bite-sized pieces
100 g / 3½ oz coriander, finely chopped (leaves and stems)
Salt and pepper
2 tsp oil, for frying

METHOD

1. Toss fish in the blacksalty seeds with some salt and pepper
2. Heat oil in a pan and stir-fry ginger and shallots. Add fish and stir-fry until cooked through
3. Stir in dragon fruit and coriander until warm

Spicy Salt Prawns

This dish can be served with chilli chutney (see recipe on page 20).

INGREDIENTS

500 g / 1 lb 2 oz large prawns, cleaned and deveined, rinsed and patted dry

2 tsp chilli flakes

1 tsp five-spice

1 tsp salt

3 tsp cornflour

200 g / 7 oz flowering garlic chives, cut into 1 cm / ⅓ in lengths (optional)

Few sprigs spring onions, cut into 1 cm / ⅓ in lengths

Oil, for frying

METHOD

1. Mix together chilli, five-spice, salt and cornflour. Coat the prawns
2. Heat oil in a pan and when very hot, stir-fry the prawns until just cooked
3. Add chives and spring onions and stir-fry for a further 2 minutes

Steamed Fish with Spicy Soy Bean Paste

The Cantonese people cook perhaps the epitome of steamed whole fish, but here the spicy soy bean paste makes it something quite Yunnan in style. For cooking at home, choose a whole fish of which you like the texture, and which is the right size for the dish which fits inside your steamer. The paste is store-bought.

INGREDIENTS

1 whole fish (e.g. barramundi, bream)
Salt, for rubbing
2 spring onions, finely chopped
1 knob ginger, finely chopped
1 tbsp spicy soy bean paste
3 stems coriander, stems finely chopped and leaves roughly chopped, keep separate
1 tbsp oil

METHOD

1. Clean fish. Score it with three diagonal crosses both ways (to end up with six scores). Rub salt into the cavity, and on the skin
2. Mix spring onion and garlic with the soy bean paste and coriander stems, and stuff into the cavity
3. Steam the fish for 10 minutes, or 15 minutes if it is thick. Remove from steamer
4. Heat oil in a saucepan. Top the fish with coriander leaves and pour the oil over the top

Pan-Fried Spicy Squid

INGREDIENTS

250 g / 9 oz squid, cleaned, ink removed, and cut into 3 cm / 1 in strips
1 tsp salt
1 tsp chilli flakes
½ tsp Sichuan peppercorns, crushed
1 clove garlic, minced
1 tsp oil, for frying

METHOD

1. Mix together the salt, chilli, peppercorns and garlic and set aside
2. Heat the oil in a pan and, over a high heat, stir-fry squid until tender. Stir in the spice mixture, cook for 1 minute, and serve immediately

THE FARMING LIFE

Government officials have just had lunch with the Song family. A simple village lunch of bitter gourd fried with Yunnan ham, battered eggplant, plain shredded squash, and starchy shredded potato spiked with green chilli.

They have come down to the banks of the Yangtze to investigate water levels. There's nothing to do, they say, but wait. These are words villagers are used to hearing.

Unlike in Beijing where, earlier in the week, flash floods caused dozens of deaths, down here it all happens slowly.

The corn is already about a metre underwater – and these plants will surely die – but the risk is that the waters will come much higher and flood the yard and even the house's courtyard or worse. The pigs, chickens and ducks (and the dog) will be moved up to higher ground – to Grandfather's house – but another tragedy potentially unfolding has to do with the new building that the Songs have just erected. It replaces a building ruined in the floods of seven years ago. They are looking cheery, he smoking and she eating a white plum, but deep down they are surely worried.

Typically of such farmers, their farm consists of cultivated plots which keep the whole family in vegetables for the year, and about six hectares of tobacco which earns the family a decent living. They receive government subsidies to plant tobacco and have built a special tower in which they dry the leaves at high temperature before they hand them over to a government office. They own three pigs, two of which last the family for a year, and the third which they can sell to a "businessman" for about 3,000 yuan. They will buy a piglet at market for about 100 yuan and fatten it up to around 300kg, and then sell that one. Unlike the Cantonese, who love to eat suckling pig, in Yunnan a suckling pig is way too precious to consume.

In such families, there is no wastage and no need to buy feed. Any leftover food, and all the vegetable peelings and fruit skins, are consumed by the animals.

An adjoining village, which hosts a weekly market, is already under water. If the waters rise in the Songs' village, they will lose almost their entire vegetable crop and some tobacco, though fortunately much of the tobacco plantings are on higher ground. One of the two daughters has plans to go to Shangri-La the next day. She is concerned about leaving her parents but knows she has to work. Her father says the trip should be no problem but she will have to take a different route. And they wait. They wait. □

RICE AND NOODLES

Cross the Bridge Noodles is probably the most famous Yunnan noodle dish (see page 200), and *mi xian* (rice noodles itself) is the most popular breakfast dish. It is served in many different-flavoured stocks, the most popular being peanut-flavoured. Introduced from the northern and eastern parts of China, the hand-cut noodles are made with eggs and flour. Many shops offer this traditional dish across Kunming, cooking the noodles quickly until they are firm and chewy (al dente). Noodles can be bought in various shapes, and also as sheets.

Bread shows up, particularly among the Hui (Chinese Muslim) ethnic minority, and as a breakfast item, especially among the Naxi people. But essentially Yunnan is rice country: white rice with meals (and mixed with potatoes) and rice noodles for breakfast.

Glutinous rice is readily available in black and red varieties in the northern parts of Yunnan where it is traditionally eaten hot (because of the cooler climate) whereas in the tropical south it is more likely to be served cold. A lovely traditional Dai dish is the steaming of glutinous rice in tubes of bamboo.

Pineapple Rice

This is an iconic Dai dish, combining two staples of the Xishuangbanna region: pineapples and rice. It is served as part of a meal even though it is quite sweet (it is not a dessert). Add sugar/honey to taste. The trick is to ensure that chunks of pineapple, rather than pineapple juice, are mixed with the rice, otherwise it will turn almost sloppy. A new trend is to add cooked peanuts (skin on); and it looks even more attractive if a combination of white and red rice is used.

INGREDIENTS

1 pineapple
½ tsp salt
115 g / 4 oz white glutinous rice, cooked
55 g / 2 oz red glutinous rice, cooked
4 tbsp sugar and/or honey

METHOD

1. To prepare the pineapple, clean it, flattening the bottom to ensure it will stand up in the steamer. Tidy up the top of the pineapple, then cut off the top and set it aside
2. Using a spoon, remove the pineapple flesh, trying to keep it in chunks. Place the flesh in a bowl with salt. If the fruit is quite sour, add sugar and/or honey at this point (up to 2 or 3 tbsp)
3. Remove the central core (this is not required for the dish). Dry out the cavity
4. Mix the pineapple flesh with the rice (the proportion should be about half-half). Spoon into the cavity almost to the top, put on the "lid", and steam for 15 minutes

Dai Noodle Soup

This is a modernised, vegetarian version of Dai noodle soup. Prepare it in a clay pot. The amounts shown are good for two bowls. Dried noodles can be substituted – cook according to the packet but take 2 minutes off the cooking time so that the noodles are al dente.

INGREDIENTS

225 g / 8 oz fresh rice noodles
1 tbsp preserved vegetables
3 shiitake mushrooms, soaked in 225 ml / 8 fl oz water, then finely sliced, soaking water reserved
½ white onion, finely sliced
1 stick celery, chopped
1 clove garlic, chopped
½ carrot, julienned
4 green beans, cut on the diagonal
3 chillies, cut in half lengthwise

METHOD

1. Half-fill a clay pot with water, bring to the boil, and add preserved vegetables, shiitake, onion, celery and garlic. Bring back to the boil, and simmer for 1 hour
2. Add carrot and beans with the mushroom water. Bring back to the boil, and simmer for 5 minutes
3. Meanwhile, blanch the noodles in hot water for 1 minute, and add to the soup with the chillies. Serve immediately

Fried Rice Noodles with Chicken

Where the Cantonese might add bean sprouts, in Yunnan flowering garlic chives might be added. Some restaurants top the noodles with Soya Chicken, using the same stock as for Braised Beef (see page 199), chopping chicken thighs and wings into small pieces, and braising for 30 minutes.

INGREDIENTS

250 g / 9 oz fresh rice noodles
1 chicken fillet, finely sliced across the grain
4 spring onions, finely chopped
2 tsp dried chilli flakes
4 chillies, roughly chopped
Mint leaves, torn
Oil, for frying

METHOD

1. Blanch the noodles in boiling water
2. Heat a little oil in a pan and stir-fry chicken for 1 minute, then add spring onions. Continue cooking for 2 minutes and then add chilli flakes. Remove to one side of the pan
3. Gently add noodles and brown a little, without stirring (they break up easily), adding a little more oil as necessary
4. Spread the meat on top, and divide among 4 bowls. Top with chillies and mint

Cold Rice Noodles with Chinese Celery & Cucumber Salad

Chinese celery is long and thin and almost white in colour, as compared with the European one which is thicker and green. Remove any fibres and dry ends, in the usual way. The addition of sesame seeds is a recent phenomena started in Kunming. It can also be made with fresh rice noodles which, if very fresh, might not be cooked at all. Sometimes tomato is used to bring a certain Dai sourness.

INGREDIENTS

300 g / 10½ oz packet dried flat rice noodles
1 tsp soy sauce • 2 tsp sesame oil
1 small red onion, finely sliced
4 stalks Chinese celery, washed and thinly sliced into 3 cm/1 in pieces
1 red pepper, cut into 3 cm / 1 in lengths
1 tsp salt • 2 tsp dried chilli flakes
1 cucumber, finely sliced into 3 cm / 1 in long pieces
2 spring onion, cut into 1 cm / ½ in long pieces
4 sprigs coriander, cut into 1 cm / ½ in long pieces
1 tsp Sichuan peppercorns, finely crushed
Sesame oil, to drizzle • 1 tbsp sesame seeds • Oil, for frying

METHOD

1. Follow the instructions on the packet to cook the noodles, but reduce cooking time by 1 minute. Drain well and season with soy sauce and sesame oil while still warm
2. Heat a little oil in a pan and fry onion, celery and red pepper until tender. Add salt and chilli flakes. Mix into noodles
3. Mix together cucumber, spring onions, coriander and peppercorns, and place on top of noodles
4. Drizzle sesame oil on top, followed by a sprinkling of sesame seeds

Akha Red Glutinous Rice with Yunnan Ham

INGREDIENTS

225 g / 8 oz red glutinous rice, cooked
150 g / 5½ oz Yunnan ham, with even amounts of lean and fat, cut into very small pieces
50 g / 1¾ oz spring onions, finely sliced
1 tsp chilli flakes
1 tsp Sichuan peppercorns
Salt and pepper, to taste

METHOD

1. Mix the rice with the ham and spring onion, with salt and pepper
2. Place in a deep earthenware mould and steam for 10 minutes

Potato Rice

This is a traditional staple for the colder northern regions of Yunnan where the quantity of rice may not be sufficient to last all year, so it is bulked up with potato. Today, the dish has become somewhat fashionable around Kunming, gentrified with the addition of little chunks of Yunnan ham (about the same quantity as the green pepper and cooked with it), and served in a handsome copper pot.

INGREDIENTS

2 potatoes, peeled and cut in 1 cm / ½ in cubes
115 g / 4 oz rice, cooked and cooled (leftover rice can be used)
1 long thin green pepper, cut into thin rings
1 red chilli, finely chopped
1 tsp salt
Oil, for deep-frying potato

METHOD

1. Heat oil in a pan and deep-fry the potato cubes until brown and crisp. Remove and drain
2. Heat a little oil in a copper pot and fry pepper and chilli with salt until aromatic
3. Stir in rice and cook until it is heated through. Add potatoes and cook until heated through.

Serve hot

Egg Fried Rice

INGREDIENTS

115 g / 4 oz rice, cooked and cooled

2 eggs, beaten

1 tomato, peeled and seeded, flesh finely cubed

4 spring onions, finely chopped

1 tsp dried chilli flakes

1 tsp salt

1 tbsp oil, for frying

METHOD

1. Heat oil and fry the rice. Set aside
2. Ensuring that the pan is only very lightly oiled, fry the egg and break it up into very small clumps
3. Stir in tomato, spring onions, chilli flakes and salt. Stir in the rice

Noodles with Fried Pork

INGREDIENTS

1 pack dried flat noodles

200 g / 7 oz pork loin, finely sliced into strips

100 g / 3½ oz Yunnan ham, about two-thirds fat, finely sliced into strips

4 stalks Chinese cabbage (or seasonal green stalks), cut into thin strips 5 cm / 2 in long

6 Chinese chives, cut into 5 cm / 2 in lengths (optional)

2 tsp oil, for frying

METHOD

1. Prepare the noodles according to the instructions on the packet, but reduce the cooking time by 1 minute
2. Heat the oil in a pan and stir-fry pork until almost done. Remove and set aside
3. Stir-fry Yunnan ham in the oil for a moment, then remove
4. Stir-fry the cabbage and cook until just done. Stir in the pork and ham, and then the noodles. Divide among 4 bowls and top with chives

Noodles with Braised Beef

Originally a Cantonese dish, braised beef served with noodles has been a tradition in Yunnan now for several decades. The addition of chillies and mint, however, is very non-Cantonese! These quantities are good for 4 bowls.

INGREDIENTS

1 pack dried flat noodles

1 large bowl braised beef (see below)

4 chillies, roughly chopped • Mint leaves, torn

METHOD

1. Prepare the noodles according to the instructions on the packet but cut back on one minute of cooking time. Divide among 4 bowls
2. Spoon beef on top, then sprinkle with chillies and mint

Braised Beef:

INGREDIENTS

500 g / 1 lb 2 oz beef shin, cut into 3 cm / 1 in cubes

1 onion, chopped • 2 star anise

2 tbsp light soy sauce • 1 tbsp dark soy sauce

1 tbsp Sichuan peppercorns

225 ml / 8 fl oz water

METHOD

1. Mix together everything except the beef
2. Bring to the boil, add meat, and simmer for about 1 hour until the beef is tender

Cross the Bridge Noodles

Cross the Bridge Noodles is quite possibly Yunnan's most famous culinary output, and very much reflects the Han Chinese style rather than the cuisines of the various ethnic minorities.

The story goes that the dish was created more than 100 years ago in Mengzi County in southeast Yunnan. A young scholar retreated each day to the peaceful Nanhu Lake to study for his imperial examinations. Every morning, his young and loving wife would prepare for him a bowl of soup noodles, and carry it across the bridge. But by the time she reached him, the soup had turned cold. What she subsequently discovered is that if she kept a layer of chicken fat on top of the soup, the soup would remain hot enough for the ingredients to be cooked in it, as she arrived.

The dish, rather like the story, has many variations, but the basic elements remain the same. More expensive versions in restaurants have the addition of more expensive ingredients. The tradition is continued in restaurants by the preparation of all manner of ingredients including finely sliced fish, pork, chicken, quail's egg, tomato and chives, laid out in individual dishes. These are cooked, pork first, in the simmering broth.

Already cooked items might include tofu skin, deep-fried pork fat and ham. Bean sprouts and the medium-size flat rice noodles are the last things to be added.

The key to a great bowl is in the chicken stock. The ultimate chicken for this is one which has plenty of yellow fat and, after being blanched, is simmered, covered, for up to four hours with a slice of ginger, a clove of garlic and a couple of spring onions (the white part only). It should fit snugly in the pan, with enough water to generously cover it. More water can be added as necessary. The clearer the soup, the better, but it should only be lightly skimmed, in order to retain that layer of fat. □

FEELING
STYLE

SNACKS AND STREET FOOD

No matter whether the weather is bracingly cold or sub-tropical hot, people in Yunnan love to eat in the open – choosing the appropriate foods to either warm up or cool down, huddling around fires or stretching out under umbrellas. Barbecue stations in particular abound on the streets, and there are always plenty of snack stalls in and around markets, selling steamed buns, crisp breads, and all kinds of pancakes. No one goes hungry at the bus stations, either.

A favourite on the streets of Jinghong after school is a little bag of sliced green mango pieces sprinkled with chilli flakes. Cubes of deep-fried potato assembled on bamboo sticks are also a favourite of school children. Barbecued cubes of tofu, and roast chestnuts and sweet potato are popular with all ages.

Potato Pancakes

INGREDIENTS

2 medium potatoes (about 250 g / 9 oz each)

Pinch salt

Oil, for frying

METHOD

1. Peel and grate the potatoes
2. Sprinkle with salt, and squeeze out any excess liquid by hand
3. Divide into 5 or 6 and create pancakes about 12 cm / 5 in wide, ½ cm / 1/5 in deep
4. Heat about 1 tbsp of oil in a pan (per pancake) and cook until lightly browned, then flip and brown the other side

Pork-stuffed Potstickers

These dumplings, which can be steamed or fried, or a combination of the two, are ubiquitous in China. The Yunnan versions are a little smaller in size and contain a larger than usual range of ingredients, flowering Chinese chives being predominant amongst those.

The recipe for making your own wraps is shown, but these can of course be readily purchased. Flour – and water – react differently in different places, particularly according to humidity levels, so work on the dough carefully; the water quantities below may not exactly work for you where you are.

FOR THE DOUGH

350 g / 12 oz flour
About 100 ml / 3½ fl oz boiling water
About 50 ml / 1¾ fl oz cold water

1. In a bowl, add boiling water to half the flour. Work the mixture with chopsticks, with fork or by hand until the flour and water are coming together in a soft, malleable form. Beware the hot dough! Turn onto a floured board and continue working. Set aside
2. Add the cold water to the remaining flour. Work similarly until a soft, malleable dough is formed
3. Combine the two doughs. Rest for about 1 hour
4. Divide the dough into four pieces and roll into cylinders of about 12 cm long x 2 cm diameter / 4¾ in x ¾ in. Divide each cylinder into small pieces, each about 7.5 g / ¼ oz in weight, the size of a small chestnut

FOR THE STUFFING

250 g / 9 oz minced pork, about one-third fat
2 tsp light soy
1-2 pinches salt
1 tsp freshly ground black pepper
1 tsp sesame oil
25 g / 1 oz flowering Chinese chives, very finely chopped
25 g / 1 oz Chinese cabbage, chopped
20 g / ¾ oz spring onion, finely chopped
20 g / ¾ oz mint, finely chopped

1. Mix together pork, soy, salt, pepper and sesame with a fork or chopsticks and place on a board
2. Slowly fold in the chopped vegetables with a chopper, folding the outsides to the insides until everything is well combined
3. Continue until the consistency is smooth and elastic. It should be moist but holding together. This process can take up to 10 minutes
4. Place a wrapper in the palm of your hand and place a heaped tsp at the centre of each wrapper. Seal the edges with 2 pleats on each side

Pumpkin Pancakes

These are like English pikelets, sold everywhere on the streets of Yunnan from Kunming to Dali to Lijiang.The consistency is very “pumpkin-ish”!

INGREDIENTS

400 g / 14 oz pumpkin
300 g / 10½ oz self raising flour, sieved
1 egg, beaten with 2 tsp sugar and a pinch of salt
100 ml / 3½ fl oz milk
100 ml water / 3½ fl oz water (reserve any remaining water after cooking the pumpkin)
Oil, for frying

METHOD

1. Place the pumpkin in a small saucepan, just cover it with water, and boil until soft. Mash thoroughly and set aside
2. Beat the egg into the flour and slowly add milk and water until the batter is thick and smooth. Combine with the pumpkin
3. Heat oil in a frying pan and spoon dollops of the mixture into it. Cook until lightly browned, then flip and lightly brown the other side

Steamed Pork Buns

In Yunnan province, it is traditional to pan-fry these little *baozi*, but with the later addition of a little water. The cabbage brings moisture to the filling. The cabbage, pork and spring onion should be in roughly the same proportions (one third, one third, one third). These buns can also be filled with a chicken-based stuffing, the recipe for which is also shown below.

INGREDIENTS

For the buns:

225 g / 8 oz self-raising flour • 1 tsp baking powder
1 tsp sugar • ½ tsp salt
110 ml / 3¾ fl oz milk
2 tsp oil or lard • Baking paper

For the filling:

150 g / 5½ oz lean pork, minced
30 g / 1¼ oz Chinese cabbage, finely shredded
20 g / ¾ oz spring onions, finely chopped
2 tsp light soy • 1 tsp sesame oil
1 tsp salt • 1 tsp pepper

2 tsp oil, for frying • 110 ml / 4 fl oz boiling water

METHOD

For the buns:

1. Put all the dry ingredients in a bowl
2. Add oil and mix, then add milk and mix, until the consistency is wet. Sit for 30 minutes

3. Cut paper into 2 cm / ¾ in squares
4. Put sufficient water into the steamer to last for 10-12 minutes

For the filling:
1. With a fork, mix the pork with the ginger, soy, sesame oil, salt and pepper. Place on a wooden board
2. Put the cabbage, chives and spring onion on top in stages and, with a chopper, begin to combine them with the pork mixture in a folding gesture, bringing the outside of the mixture into the middle
3. Continue this process for up to 10 minutes until the mixture is smooth, sticky, and elastic. It should be moist but hold together. The consistency is very important

To assemble the buns:
1. On a floured surface, break dough into golf ball-sized pieces and flatten in the palm of your hand into a circle. Place a heaped tsp of the pork mixture in the centre
2. Fold into a semi-circle, sealing the edges with two pleats on each side

To cook the buns:
1. Heat the oil in a pan and, when sizzling, carefully place the buns
2. After 2 minutes the oil will begin to caramelise. Add boiling water, cover, and turn the heat down to medium. Cook for about 6 minutes until transparent, and browned on the bottom

Alternative filling recipe with chicken:
250 g / 9 oz chicken, minced
½ bamboo shoot (canned), about 5 cm / 2 in piece, finely chopped
6 dried Chinese mushrooms, soaked in warm water, finely chopped
5 cm / 2 in piece ginger, finely chopped
2 medium shallots, finely chopped • 1 spring onion, finely chopped
4 leaves cabbage (about 25 g / 1 oz), finely chopped
1 tsp soy sauce • 1 tsp black pepper • ½ tsp salt

Crispy Spring Onion Cakes

INGREDIENTS

450 g / 1 lb plain flour
1 tsp salt
300 ml / ½ pint boiling water
1 tbsp cold water
50 g / 1¾ oz lard
150 g / 5½ oz spring onions, roughly chopped
Sea salt, for sprinkling
Oil, for frying

METHOD

1. Sift the flour and salt into a bowl, stir in the boiling water. Add the cold water and, when sufficiently cool, knead the dough until thick and smooth. Place in a bowl, cover with a damp cloth, and leave for at least 20 minutes
2. Knead the dough for a couple of minutes and divide into 12 pieces. Roll out each piece until thin. Smear with lard, dot with spring onion, and sprinkle with sea salt. Reform into a ball, and roll out again in a 10 cm / 4 in diameter circle
3. Heat 1 tsp of oil in a frying pan, and fry one pancake at a time for 3 minutes on each side until beginning to brown, gently squashing it into the oil to ensure a smooth surface. Shake the pan from time to time. Serve immediately

Spring Onion Pancakes

INGREDIENTS

4 tbsp finely chopped spring onions
200 g / 7 oz plain flour
1 tsp salt
2 eggs
2 egg yolks
400 ml / 14 fl oz milk
200 ml / 7 oz water
3 tbsp oil
Oil, for frying

METHOD

1. Heat a little oil in a pan and stir-fry the spring onion until beginning to soften. Remove and set aside
2. Sieve the flour and salt into a bowl. Beat the eggs with the egg yolks, and mix into the flour
3. Slowly add the milk and water, beating vigorously, until the batter is creamy. Stir in 3 tbsp of oil and continue beating. Stir in the spring onions
4. Into a hot pan, pour in about 1 tbsp of the batter and cook until set but not browned. Turn (optional)

Dinner at Gold Beach

It's the eve, in tropical Xishuangbanna, of the final Chinese New Year celebration – Red Lantern Festival. Jinghong, meaning "City of Dawn" in the ethnic minority Dai language, is abuzz this Saturday evening with people criss-crossing the main roads and pausing at tiny hawker stalls. Extended family groups mingle at the food booths in the park, situated alongside the Mekong River, enjoying the cooler temperatures which follow sundown. The special dish to be shared for this festival is *tang yuan*: small balls made of glutinous rice flour (white or red, depending on which coloured rice they have been made from), flavoured with black sesame and served in a sugar syrup. Like many Chinese New Year dishes, their name renders them auspicious. In this case, they represent the expectation of the family to gather again, together.

The first full moon (the Chinese calendar is of course based on the movements of the moon) of the year, on this clear and balmy night, shimmers over the Lanna-esque roofs, the life-size elephant statues, and tropical tree-lined boulevards which give the small but ever-expanding city of Jinghong its unique Southeast Asian character. Red lanterns of all sizes, hanging from trees, lamp posts and shop fronts, flutter in a gentle breeze.

The city is also abuzz in a drink-and-dine destination just a stone's throw from this park by the Mekong. Here, in the lively "Gold Beach" zone, al fresco beer and barbecue are the year-round traditions. There's a lively nightlife in Jinghong these days, where the locals hang. In the same way that Hong Kong's trendy Lan Kwai Fong district morphed in 20 years from a hangout for expatriates and tourists to a destination for locals, so are things changing in this city, and in many mainland China cities way beyond Beijing and Shanghai.

At Gold Beach, restaurants and bars spill onto the streets; worn wooden tables and wooden benches are laid out among the trees which twinkle with fairy lights (there's very little street lighting). Rap emanates from one or two bars. Gentle strands of smoke rise above charcoal barbecues set up on the pavements, preparing typical Dai skewers of meat, of fish, of seafood, of tofu, of vegetables.

On one corner, Beer City bar serves the local aberrant Tsingtao beer mixed with pineapple juice in huge mugs with their own little taps, around which gather groups of young people chatting and smoking, or playing cards. They snack on their favourite skewers

– the local delicacy of buffalo skin dipped into a fiery sauce of ginger, garlic and chilli. There are multi-generational families too, ordering food, because Beer City is also a Dai restaurant of repute.

One of the owners, a no-nonsense Chinese who typically works from four in the afternoon until two in the morning, stops to chat to one table. They've two pets with them, one a little brown poodle and the other, on a lead, a bright white and clearly well fed and domesticated ferret. She picks up the rat-like animal, who takes this attention meekly.

Dishes begin to arrive, in no particular order, but in quick succession. It's not easy to make out what they are in the barely-there outdoor lighting. Dai grilled fish with lemon, and pineapple rice, are two of the most popular dishes here – as are crinkly fried potato chips, to be dipped in ground chilli! Further, sweet potato patties are dipped into a thick sauce made from condensed milk. But other dishes are more obviously Dai such as the sour and spicy, deeply coloured soup dotted with pieces of green bean cake. A crunchy sliced cucumber salad is a simple but beautifully executed demonstration of how to create a subtle backdrop of ginger, garlic and chilli while coming across as fresh. There's battered stinky tofu, a pungent soy and mustard dip (the latter like an extra strong wasabi), little bits of fried squid, and fresh soy beans for shelling to snack on.

Having returned the furry ferret to the owner's lap, the night's hostess is unashamedly commenting on another female guest's ears. Large lobes mean luck and fortune. In a man, they're even more highly desirable if a woman seeks a comfortable life. Grab those ears. □

CHEESE

Contrary to popular opinion, there's a long history of cheese eating in China, though only among certain (mostly nomadic) peoples, and in certain provinces. Nowhere is cheese more traditional than in Yunnan, where it is made with cow, goat and yak milk. It is often served at festivals and at marriage banquets. In markets in Yunnan, whole stalls are piled high with it, including pyramids of softly smoked yak cheese, strips or cubes of dried cheese, and large packs of soft cheese. It can be bought on the street as a snack, and restaurants serve it, often deep-fried. Yunnan goat cheese has only been enjoyed over the years by local people, ameliorated with a sprinkling of sugar.

There has been quite a movement over the years to help improve cheese quality, and to bring it to international (export) standards. There is even the occasional farm devoted to the production of Western-style cheeses made from cow's milk. Across the province there are good dairy farms, from Lijiang to Lincang to Dali; and some say the best goat cheese comes from the black goat of the Stone Forest, about one hour outside Kunming.

Rushan is sold in long sheets, somewhat resembling beancurd skin, and is fried. The oil temperature has to be just right: too hot and the cheese burns. At the correct temperature, it fluffs up, and is served with sugar or honey. *Rubing* is made from goat milk, and is also sliced and fried. String cheese is also a popular product. In Dali, cheese is a street snack; in Shangri-La, the whey part (left over after the butter is made) is deep-fried in little balls, with a slightly sour taste.

Fried Yunnan Goat Cheese with Tomato Salsa

Yunnan goat cheese has not been anything much over the years, tasting at best sour and at worst neutral. But the locals love their cheese. For this dish, substitute Halloumi or Dutch goat cheese, which have a similar texture, though the taste is not the same. Serve with tomato salsa (see recipe on page 24), chilli chutney (page 20) or spicy salt (page 24).

INGREDIENTS

150 g / 5½ oz goat cheese

1 tsp oil

METHOD

1. Slice the cheese to desired thickness
2. Place a cast iron pan on a medium heat and brush the oil evenly across it
3. Fry cheese slices on both sides until golden brown

Yunnan Ham with Broad Beans & Goat Cheese

Any kind of seasonal beans can be used for this Bai dish. The beans absorb the flavours of the ham. Use mild Gouda as a substitute for *Rubing*.

INGREDIENTS

25 g / 1 oz Yunnan ham, both lean and fat, thinly sliced
2 cloves garlic, crushed
1 shallot, crushed
100 g / 3½ oz broad beans (shelled weight)
50 ml / 1¾ fl oz water
100 g / 3½ oz goat cheese (*Rubing*), cut to double the size of the beans
1 tsp Sichuan peppercorns
Salt, to taste

METHOD

1. Render the ham fat in a pan over a medium-hot flame until the fat is translucent. Remove the lean ham, and set aside
2. Using the rendered ham fat, stir-fry the garlic and shallot with the beans for 2 minutes, add a little water, cover, and cook for about 5 minutes until the beans are tender
3. Stir in ham and cheese, sprinkle with peppercorns and salt

Goat Cheese with Peas and Snake Beans

Substitute with Halloumi if you do not have access to Yunnan goat cheese, or a Dutch goat cheese with a Gouda-like texture. This dish should finish quite dry.

INGREDIENTS

200 g / 7 oz goat cheese, cut into very small cubes (slightly larger than a pea)
200 g / 7 oz fresh shelled peas (do not use frozen)
200 g / 7 oz snake beans, sliced into pieces slightly larger than a pea
1 clove garlic, crushed
1 tbsp oil
4 tbsp water

METHOD

1. Heat the oil and fry the garlic until just translucent. Stir in the peas and beans
2. Add the cheese and fry for a minute
3. Pour in the water, cover, and simmer for 1 minute

The Wa Cheesemaker

As little as 25 years ago, the land around the inland city of Lincang was jungle, populated by bears and tigers. This area is home to the Wa ethnic minority, a largely mountain-dwelling people with high rates of illiteracy and various connected problems.

A tree replanting scheme was started some 15 years ago, together with training programmes for the Wa in not only language but pig and cow husbandry, too. At a dairy farm close to Lincang airport, Am Pleek learnt how to make cheese – the Western way – and now she's training up an assistant and helping take care of the young girls who live in the dormitory and work on the farm. They refer to her as "Big Mama." It is a tremendous experience and a chance for everyone to learn marketable skills.

Am Pleek is talking about her earliest food memories: her father going hunting, for example. To this day she loves game, rabbit, rodents and squirrel. Also the rice bird soup, for which you roll the bird in the fire to remove the feathers, but don't wash it because it will lose its distinctive bird flavour. Chop it into a broth with lots of garlic and chilli. Actually, she still sees that little bird around, even today.

One of her earliest culinary memories with her mother revolves around the annual grasshopper cycle. The young ones can be harvested from the mountainside twice a year, but the winter harvest is preferred because then they've already released their eggs and the intestines are cleaner. These "sweet" hoppers are boiled with chillies and herbs to create a soup which is a true delicacy in local culture.

There's little in common with the cuisines of other ethnic minorities, says Am Pleek, because there are so many wild vegetables and herbs on the mountainsides which simply don't grow anywhere else. The chickens live on the mountains too, fed on rice and corn – good, clean food. Chickens are important in Wa culture: the "medicine man" will inspect the chicken's tongue to see what it is "saying". Good or bad, it can be eaten anyway!

Wa is probably the most spicy (and salty) of the cuisines of the ethnic minorities. Even the rice porridge called *moik*, made with chicken, vegetables and cilantro, is intensely fiery. Herbs like saw leaf (which the Wa call "fish gill herb") are extensively used with chicken, with fish, and with cow intestine. Mint and *rau ram* show up often, too, both of which the Wa believe make fish "less fishy".

Typically, young Wa people leave home and journey for up to a week to the east coast of China to work in factories, in the process losing their cultural identity. Am Pleek saw in the dairy and cheese-

making industries a way for young people to stay in their community while earning a decent living.

At first, she would only eat the Mozzarella and string cheeses because they tasted "fresh" to her. The smell of Cheddar would shrivel her face like a raisin! Today, she appreciates the different flavours of Feta, Gouda and Gruyère, paired with fruits and nuts – and sometimes drizzled with honey produced right there on the mountainside. ☐

DESSERTS

For all the exotic cooking of the ethnic minorities, Yunnan is no different from the rest of China when it comes to the development of the dessert. Nor though are the nearby countries of southeast Asia famous for desserts beyond concoctions based usually on glutinous rice and coconut milk.

The Chinese in general eat fruit as a snack, rather than as dessert immediately after a meal – and in this context Yunnan is the ultimate destination. Crowds gather at fruit stalls in the evenings to while away the time drinking tea and enjoying whatever is in season. And there's always something in season.

So by way of dessert, serve bunches of grapes, or bowls of lychees and longans, or simply create a fruit platter with the brightest-coloured fruit you can find. Or take lovely fruit like ripe bananas and make stuffed sweet crepes.

Red Bean and Sweet Potato Balls

INGREDIENTS

200 g / 7 oz sweet potatoes (2 medium sized)
50 g / 1¾ oz self-raising flour
1 egg, beaten
2 tsp sugar
Salt, to taste
Small packet red bean paste
Sesame seeds, for coating
Oil, for frying

METHOD

1. Cover sweet potato in a pan with water, bring to the boil and simmer for 40 minutes. Cool and remove skin. Mash with a fork, add sugar and salt
2. Fold the flour into the egg and combine with the sweet potato. Form into a soft dough and divide in two. Roll each piece into a cylinder about 2 cm / ¾ in diameter. Cut into 2 cm / ¾ in pieces and roll into balls
3. Press thumb into ball to make a hole, and fill it with 1 tsp red bean paste. Pinch edges together to enclose the paste, and re-form into a ball. Roll in sesame seeds
4. Shallow-fry in medium hot oil for 2 minutes on each side. Drain on paper towels and serve hot or cold

Pumpkin & Black Glutinous Rice Soup

This dish is often prepared for village wedding celebrations, the sugar added to make it an appropriate "closing" dish. Sweet potato and yam, traditional Yunnan favourites, could also be used. A more modern version of this simple dessert would add in about 100 g / 3½ oz of sago at the same time as the pumpkin. The consistency should be thick but still soupy.

INGREDIENTS

350 g / 12 oz black glutinous rice, washed
½ tsp salt
200 g / 7 oz pumpkin, peeled and cut into 5 cm / 2 in square chunks
4 tbsp brown sugar, or to taste

METHOD

1. Half-fill a large pot with water, bring to the boil, add rice and salt. Simmer for about 30 minutes until very thick. If all the water has evaporated, add about 200 ml / 7 fl oz more
2. Add pumpkin and, when very tender, stir in the sugar

In the Nomau Xichang Market

Pinch yourself, this gloriously sunny February morning at just after 10 o'clock, or you might imagine you were wandering in a wet market in the south of Vietnam – or Laos, even Thailand.

The edible scenery begins with herbs in multiple hues of green – basil, coriander, saw leaf herb (also known as long coriander), Vietnamese *rau ram* – and in multiple varieties of something as simple as mint. A small bunch of Asian herbs which might, in cities from London to Hong Kong, be sold in a little plastic pack at great expense, is here overflowing from baskets and sold for a child's loose change.

There are piles of green papayas and green mangoes, which form the base for so many salads from Myanmar, Thailand and Vietnam, together with pink-tinged banana blossom. Next, long purple eggplants, small round green-and-white striped ones, and the sprigs of tiny green ones, no bigger than a pea, which show up in so many Thai curries.

The Nomau Xichang market in Jinghong city, then, is a pertinent reminder that country borders are arbitrary. Rarely based on geography, they're largely to do with politics and religion and, before that, at least

in this part of the world, on kingdoms. Those borders, though, may well become validated culturally, with an ethnic minority living on two sides of the same mountain, in two different countries. Agriculture can be manipulated by government and by economics, but people tend to eat what they were brought up on and, traditionally, what they are able to grow on their own little piece of land. And so it is that this covered downtown market, once muddy and littered, but now tiled underfoot with workers employed to sweep its ample aisles, evokes those of the southeast Asian countries that Xishuangbanna borders.

This whitewashed section with gleaming floors is systematic. Here people shop for shoes and toiletries, and vendors' kids roam around, offered nuts and candies. One vendor works on her embroidery while her neighbour taps away on his computer. Another, behind the most enormous piles of limes you've ever seen (and she's quite enormous herself), has abandoned herself to whatever she's listening to on her headphones. She reluctantly serves someone. Another is gesturing: buy limes from me instead! It's a riot of colour from the brilliant red of the chillies to the brilliant yellow of the quinces.

It is less orderly in the adjoining area where peas are being shelled, beans are being podded, corn kernels are cut off the cob, and bamboo is shredded. There's a woman squatting with just a few bunches of herbs and some cabbages in front of her. No rented market stall for her. Buy that produce and you'd feel that you were eating the produce of a village garden. Timid personalities from the countryside juxtapose urbanites with the easy confidence of insurance salesmen. It's chaotic in the fish and seafood section, with choppers hitting wooden boards and showers of scales hitting the rough floor.

There are changes afoot for Jinghong's food culture. An orderly Taiwan-owned supermarket has just opened, and there's now a KFC, the first in this city. What becomes of the markets in the face of these changes?

Right now, Yunnan is producing the most good, clean and fair (to borrow a description from the Slow Food movement) produce in the whole of China. More than ever, we need to know what we are eating, and to be able to trust our food. Market produce is seasonal, putting consumers in touch with nature, and is part of the rhythm of life.

In markets such as those in Jinghong, the connections between the farmer or vendor and the consumer are almost mystical, because of animist relationships with the mountains, the trees; the river and the sky. So this produce speaks of the connection of man and the environment; of the connection of man and appropriate food; of a connection, based on trust, between vendor and consumer.

The market must stay. □

Acknowledgements

What an amazing journey I have had with Annabel while creating this cookbook, and I hope that you will enjoy the journey with us as you read the stories about the food culture and the people Annabel meets – and as you cook the recipes which are my take on Yunnan cuisine.

For me, the journey started with creating dishes in Annabel's kitchen and presenting Yunnan produce to her guests, and it was their positive feedback which gave rise to Annabel writing up the recipes. So in fact we could say that this book began when we started to showcase the regional produce of Yunnan. You will find that there are a good number of recipes which are rich in colour and this reflects the wonderful variety of vegetables. All the dishes are rich in flavour because of Yunnan's diverse climate and ethnic cultures.

Living in Yunnan since 2002 has exposed me to the Dai food culture, and it is this which first excited Annabel's palate. The journey continued with my cooking for her the many different ways of bringing spicy and sour flavours together, and these dishes are also included in this book.

However, my ability to create a dish comes from much discussion and tastings with friends. Thanks to Irene Dung who engaged me with her *Rubing* Yunnan goat cheese. To Ping Ping Shi from Lijiang who welcomed me into her project to produce clean and nutritious food. To Christina Duan in Kunming who shared local food from her hometown near Dali. To Cammy Yiu who gave very constructive and positive feedback on the dishes I cooked in Hong Kong. To San Lin who inspired me with his amazing photography. And to my mother who is my inspiration – the best at creating a dish.

– Linda Chia

Bless you, Ugo and Chiara: you introduced me to Linda!

Thanks to all those who gave me such insights into Yunnan life. In Jinghong – Orchid, owner of Mei Mei Café. In Dali – Luxi Yuan, owner of cooking school Rice & Friends; and Joshe (he only has one name), tour guide and remarkable cultural commentator for someone so young.

In Lijiang – Aw Hwee Ling, owner of the delightful boutique hotel Bivou, and her crew. In Kunming, so many thanks to Charlie, Jeff, Tony, Yiran, Tommy the driver and all the crowd at Angsana Fuxian Lake for such fun. Also thanks to my former Macau IFT Wine Studies student, Cornell Wu, and his father, for the Yunnan Red experience. In Yiliang, thanks to Andrew

Chen (also from IFT) and his extended family for welcoming me so warmly to their guesthouse, and for taking me mushroom foraging.

In Hong Kong, many thanks to hotel supplier Equip Asia, a subsidiary of Chiram Strategic, which loaned much of the table-top ware featured in the recipe shots. And to all the people who tirelessly tasted, including the Slow Food gang: Walter Kern, Terrence Annamunthodo, Diane Espley, Doris Lau, Yale Wang and Ceri Sherlock. To Ping Ping for hand-delivering the Nujiang ham! To Stephen Quinn for the video clips; and Grace Belicena for her unbelievable help in the kitchen.

– Annabel Jackson